Overcoming Anxiety at Work

Vincent Miskell and Jane R. Miskell

The Business Skills Express Series

BUSINESS ONE IRWIN/MIRROR PRESS
Burr Ridge, Illinois
New York, New York
Boston, Massachusetts

This publication is designed to provide accurate and authoritative information in regard to the subject matter covered. It is sold with the understanding that neither the author nor the publisher is engaged in rendering legal, accounting, or other professional service. If legal advice or other expert assistance is required, the services of a competent professional person should be sought.

From a Declaration of Principles jointly adopted by a Committee of the American Bar Association and a Committee of Publishers.

Mirror Press: David R. Helmstadter
                                  Carla F. Tishler

Editor-in-Chief: Jeffrey A. Krames
Project editor: Stephanie M. Britt
Production manager: Diane Palmer
Designer: Jeanne M. Rivera
Art coordinator: Heather Burbridge
Illustrator: Boston Graphics, Inc.
Compositor: Alexander Graphics
Typeface: 12/14 Criterion
Printer: Malloy Lithographing, Inc.

Library of Congress Cataloging-in-Publication Data

Miskell, Vincent.
    Overcoming anxiety at work / by Vincent Miskell and Jane R. Miskell.
        p.   cm. -- (Business skills express)
    Includes bibliographical references.
    ISBN 1-55623-869-X
    1. Job stress.   2. Anxiety.   3. Stress management.   I. Miskell. Jane R.   II. Title.
    HF5548.85.M57   1994
    158.7—dc20   93–12077

Printed in the United States of America
1 2 3 4 5 6 7 8 9 0   ML   0 9 8 7 6 5 4 3

PREFACE

Anxiety on the job can cause many people to miss career opportunities or the satisfactions and benefits that hard work brings.

Temporarily, people may avoid the symptoms of anxiety—the racing heartbeat, the rapid shallow breathing, the jittery stomach, the trembling speech, and scattered thoughts. But their maneuvers and short-term distractions usually lead to more worries, poorer performance, and increased anxiety, plus further limit their chances for on-the-job success and long-term career satisfaction.

By practicing the Inventory-Insight-Action (I-I-A) process of *Overcoming Anxiety at Work*, you will learn to free yourself from the fear reactions that prevent you from doing your best work. This book presents exercises that will keep you calm under stress and encourage you to act more boldly in anxiety-provoking situations.

Even before you reach the end of the book, you should be able to act more confidently in tense or negative employment situations. By setting aside time every day to practice the I-I-A process, you can overcome anxiety at work.

Vincent Miskell
Jane R. Miskell

Please note that although the I-I-A method is effective at reducing some anxieties, people with very serious anxieties may want to consult a doctor or therapist.

ABOUT THE AUTHORS

Vincent Miskell is an educator and trainer in the New York area. Drawing on his professional experience as a supervisor and instructor, Mr. Miskell has formulated an approach to dealing with anxiety in the workplace and implements this approach in training seminars and workshops. He is currently Coordinator of Academic Administration at Technical Career Institutes in New York.

Jane R. Miskell is an educator and consultant specializing in motivation techniques, stress management, diversity awareness, study skills, and curriculum development. Her clients and affiliations include the United States Navy, California State Prison, Camarillo State Youth Authority, Ventura College, the New School for Social Research, Sterling Associates, and North American Training Inc. Ms. Miskell is currently the Associate Dean for Student Affairs at Technical Career Institutes in New York.

ABOUT
BUSINESS ONE IRWIN

Business One Irwin is the nation's premier publisher of business books. As a Times Mirror company, we work closely with Times Mirror training organizations, including Zenger-Miller, Inc., Learning International, Inc., and Kaset International, to serve the training needs of business and industry.

About the Business Skills Express Series

This expanding series of authoritative, concise, and fast-paced books delivers high quality training on key business topics at a remarkably affordable cost. The series will help managers, supervisors, and front line personnel in organizations of all sizes and types hone their business skills while enhancing job performance and career satisfaction.

Business Skills Express books are ideal for employee seminars, independent self-study, on-the-job training, and classroom-based instruction. Express books are also convenient-to-use references at work.

CONTENTS

Self-Assessment

PRELIMINARY ANXIETY READING

Get a basic reading on your anxiety levels at home and at work. For each question, give a score for yourself *at home* and another score for yourself *at work*.

Score four, when your answer is *frequently* or *always*.

Score two, when your answer is *sometimes*.

Score zero, when your answer is *never* or *almost never*.

	At Home	At Work
Group I. I feel anxious when:		
1. I'm late.		4
2. I might make a mistake.		2
3. I'm being criticized.		
4. I'm being watched while working.		0
5. I think about losing control.		0
Subtotals		

	At Home	At Work
Group II. I feel anxious when:		
6. Speaking to those in authority.		0
7. Speaking to a small group.		0
8. Speaking to a large group.		4
9. Speaking on the telephone.		0
10. Speaking to strangers.		2
Subtotals		

	At Home	At Work
Group III. I feel anxious when:		
11. I get angry.	2	2
12. Confronting those who are negligent.	0	0
13. Dealing with bossy people.	0	2
14. Dealing with angry people.	2	4
15. Thinking about being attacked.	0	4
Subtotals		

	At Home	At Work
Group IV. I feel anxious when:		
16. I have to change a routine or plan.	0	0
17. Thinking about injury or illness.	0	0
18. Taking on new responsibilities.	2	2
19. Meeting deadlines.	0	2
20. Learning to use new equipment.	0	0
Subtotals		

	At Home	At Work
Group V. I feel anxious when:		
21. I'm surrounded by a crowd.	0	0
22. I'm completely alone.	0	0
23. I'm in enclosed places.	0	0
24. I hear a sudden loud noise.	0	0
25. I hear sirens.	0	0
Subtotals		

	At Home	At Work
Total scores	6	26

32

1 | Jitters on the Job

This chapter will help you to:

- Create targets for change.
- Learn your anxiety score.
- Have a complete anxiety profile.

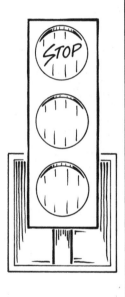

This is an inventory chapter. Stop and take stock of your situation. It is the first step toward overcoming anxiety. It is natural to feel afraid, anxious, and worried in certain circumstances. Unfortunately, automatic fear reactions are frequently triggered by situations that are not really threatening. People can learn to resist anxious feelings and risk the unknown dangers of the outside world. Humans develop courage and confidence while doing most of the tasks they choose (or are compelled) to do.

The workplace, with its special performance rules, competitiveness, and struggles for profit or productivity, regularly sets off fear reactions. Depending on work habits and responsibilities, courage and confidence can vary greatly from task to task.

The company hero, who fought an unfair tax ruling and saved hundreds of jobs, is too frightened to make a short presentation to a meeting of department heads. A secretary who negotiates meeting schedules, credit terms, and production deadlines gets migraine headaches when even thinking about asking for a few extra days off. ∎

INVENTORY-INSIGHT-ACTION

Use this easy-to-remember three-step process to help overcome your particular workplace anxieties. Think about this process in various ways:

Inventory—Insight—Action

I-I-A

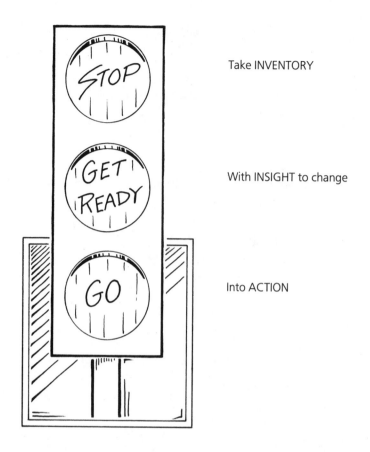

Take INVENTORY

With INSIGHT to change

Into ACTION

It's probably easiest to visualize the three steps as a traffic light.

Most problems can be handled by employing the I-I-A process. This book will attempt to solve the problem of inappropriate anxiety at work by employing the Inventory-Insight-Action process in a series of steps.

COMPLETING YOUR INVENTORY

Before reviewing the results of the self-assessment that you filled out before this chapter, you'll need to look at your physical reactions to anxiety at work. Try to be as objective as possible as you weigh the impact of fear reactions on your physical state.

Physical Inventory

Choose *rarely* if you never or almost never experience discomfort or disruption.

Pick *sometimes* if you experience problems occasionally.

Check off *frequently* if you always or almost always have difficulties.

I. Voice, Throat, and Mouth	Rarely	Sometimes	Frequently
1. Pitch too high.	☐	☐	☐
2. Volume too low.	☐	☐	☐
3. Speech too rapid.	☐	☐	☐
4. Halting speech.	☐	☐	☐
5. Trembling voice.	☐	☐	☐
6. Stammer.	☐	☐	☐
7. Monotone voice.	☐	☐	☐
8. Lump in throat.	☐	☐	☐
9. Dry mouth.	☐	☐	☐
10. Choking sensation.	☐	☐	☐

II. Lower Body and Chest	Rarely	Sometimes	Frequently
1. Stomach cramps.	☐	☐	☐
2. Butterflies.	☐	☐	☐
3. Nausea.	☐	☐	☐
4. Diarrhea.	☐	☐	☐
5. Frequent urination.	☐	☐	☐
6. Pounding heart.	☐	☐	☐
7. Chest pain.	☐	☐	☐
8. Palpitations.	☐	☐	☐
9. Rapid breathing.	☐	☐	☐
10. Gasping for air.	☐	☐	☐

III. Head, Neck, and Face	Rarely	Sometimes	Frequently
1. Dizziness.	☐	☐	☐
2. Headaches or migraines.	☐	☐	☐
3. Eye pain or irritation.	☐	☐	☐
4. Blurry vision.	☐	☐	☐
5. Neck ache.	☐	☐	☐
6. Furrowed brow.	☐	☐	☐
7. Stony or dead face.	☐	☐	☐
8. Sad or scared face.	☐	☐	☐

	Rarely	Sometimes	Frequently
9. Pale, flushed, or hot face.	☐	☐	☐
10. Facial tics.	☐	☐	☐

IV. Whole Body and Limbs	Rarely	Sometimes	Frequently
1. Excessive sweating.	☐	☐	☐
2. Shaky legs or hands.	☐	☐	☐
3. Awkwardness.	☐	☐	☐
4. Loss of balance.	☐	☐	☐
5. Unable to be still.	☐	☐	☐
6. Feeling weak or faint.	☐	☐	☐
7. Feverish.	☐	☐	☐
8. Frozen in place.	☐	☐	☐
9. Jittery.	☐	☐	☐
10. Sleepy.	☐	☐	☐

V. Other Physical Problems **(Fill in any missing discomforts.)**	Rarely	Sometimes	Frequently
1. _____	☐	☐	☐
2. _____	☐	☐	☐
3. _____	☐	☐	☐
4. _____	☐	☐	☐
5. _____	☐	☐	☐
6. _____	☐	☐	☐
7. _____	☐	☐	☐
8. _____	☐	☐	☐
9. _____	☐	☐	☐
10. _____	☐	☐	☐

Targets for Change

By filling in scores for the Preliminary Anxiety Reading and checking off items in the Physical Inventory, you've begun to form a truly objective picture of your anxiety reactions. Forming a clear picture of your anxiety-provoking situations and your physical discomforts, amounts to constructing an anxiety profile. It creates specific targets for change.

Your Basic Anxiety Level

Using your at home total on the Preliminary Anxiety Reading as a baseline, you can reach certain conclusions about your confidence levels at work. In general, at home scores are usually lower than those at work. There are many circumstances in which at home difficulties can affect at work anxiety levels and vice versa. Those cases will be explored later. At this point, assume that at work difficulties are the main sources of workplace anxiety.

Some of you may have only a few high scores and appear to be more confident than you feel. Objectively, a low overall at work score probably means that you are a great deal more confident than you realize in most areas of your job. In any case, your at work scores will help you target those specific areas that need change. Look at your total at work score and find its range among the scores listed.

Total scores of eight or less at work are low.   Your overall anxiety level appears so low that you should function very well with many job responsibilities that are perhaps expanding. Any at work anxieties that are blocking your progress can be immediately targeted and changed. Your confidence is high enough to get you through any difficulties. Try to transfer some of the courage from your high-confidence areas to your anxiety area(s). We'll show you how in this book. Delay your push for advancement only if using a specific job skill (such as public speaking) is both mandatory for the new assignment and absolutely terrifying for you to perform. Otherwise, you can practice the I-I-A method, as you go along, on any new problems created by more challenging assignments.

Total scores of 10 to 28 at work are moderate.   You show high potential and confidence but still have doubts and anxieties about your ability to learn new skills. Maybe a particular job situation directly blocks your advancement or makes your present work unpleasant in some way. By building on your strengths and applying the I-I-A method to weaker areas, you can overcome the few anxiety barriers that remain in your way.

Total scores of 30 to 50 at work are moderately high.   Anxiety blocks your ability part of the time to take advantage of opportunities for advancement and it creates job discomfort. You probably avoid particular kinds of work or suffer through those you can't pass on to others. The I-I-A method can help you in two ways: It will provide you with courage to take on new assignments. Step-by-step, it will also help you gain the confidence to feel better about the tasks that you must handle on the job now.

1

Total Scores above 50 at work are high.   Your high score indicates that being on the job is not very comfortable for you and you need to work on several different areas at once. Perhaps a recent change (a new job or a new supervisor) is causing the high anxiety reading. Whatever the cause, devote as much time as you can to doing the exercises and following the programs. You need to concentrate on bringing your overall level of anxiety down and becoming more comfortable with your present on-the-job tasks. Give the I-I-A process a chance to work by following it faithfully for a few weeks.

At Home Scores

If at home totals are the same or nearly the same as at work totals, job situation may have little to do with the overall anxiety level. Inherited disposition, temperament, or lifestyle may be the determining factor in the scores. (An extreme work situation may greatly increase at home totals as well. In such cases, the at home scores should be discounted, and the at work anxieties targeted immediately.) Fortunately, the inventory-insight-action program will work just as effectively on at home anxieties as on those experienced on the job, so if your totals are similar for at home and at work, use the I-I-A method on both.

Most employees have lower at home totals and lower individual scores for performing the same tasks. You may have scored a zero at home for meeting deadlines—such as paying bills on time—but scored as much as four, the maximum, for meeting deadlines—paying company bills—at work. Why are you confident, almost completely free of anxiety, at home but sweating bullets at work in relatively the same situation? The stakes are higher, but why leap from zero to the top of the scale? Why would someone with a total anxiety score of 20 at home, for instance, rocket up to 60 for an at work total?

Later chapters will answer these questions. It is important to realize now that if you actually have little or no anxiety while performing certain tasks outside of work, then you should also be able to perform those same or similar tasks at work with little or no anxiety.

Groups I through V

The 25 items used to determine your anxiety level are divided into five broad categories:

Category	Description
Group I	Negative evaluation, failure, and external- and self-scrutiny.
Group II	Public speaking, speaking up, and self-expression.
Group III	Aggression, anger, and self-defense.
Group IV	Initiating and adapting to change.
Group V	Physical environment.

Those groups with the highest subtotals are natural targets for change, although particular items from each group may need special efforts. To round out your anxiety profile, you need to combine the results of the Self-Assessment (Preliminary Anxiety Reading) with the Physical Inventory.

Anxiety Profile

Working through each group, match the items that you scored two or four with those physical reactions that were checked *sometimes* or *frequently*. (Unless necessary, omit items scored zero and physical reactions checked *rarely*.)

Group I: Negative evaluation, failure, and external- and self-scrutiny.

Item	Physical Discomfort

Group II: Public speaking, speaking up, and self-expression.

Item	Physical Discomfort

Item	Physical Discomfort

Group III: Aggression, anger, and self-defense.

Item	Physical Discomfort

Group IV: Initiating and adapting to change.

Item	Physical Discomfort

Group V: Physical environment.

Item	Physical Discomfort

Chapter Checkpoints

✓ Fear reactions are natural.

✓ At home anxiety scores are usually lower than at work scores.

✓ Your anxiety profile is the first step toward overcoming anxiety at work through the Inventory-Insight-Action process.

2 | Anxiety Insights

This chapter will help you to:

- Learn about anxiety reactions.
- Realize that biology is only the beginning.
- Understand the difference between your reactions and your responses.

This is an insight chapter designed to help look closer at what you discovered in Chapter 1.

Insight is an important step toward change, though rarely adequate by itself. Knowing why people react the way they do and knowing that others share in the same experiences often brings relief. At least people know they are not alone.

ANXIETY REACTION 1: FIGHT-FLIGHT

Huddled together with three others, tension passes through you like electricity while you wait. "Ahh!" someone screams the signal and you're up on your feet running with a sudden burst of energy surging throughout your body. Your breath catches fire in your chest as you sweep with the others like a wind across the open field. . . . ■

This scene might be from a war novel, a Western movie, or some other adventure that stirs the blood and stimulates the imagination. It might have been from a real life-and-death situation about 100,000 years ago when people first roamed in tribal bands over the earth. Emergency energy was essential for survival, and those whose bodies supplied enough adrenaline to help them fight fiercely or flee in terror lived to pass on these abilities to their descendants.

This fight-flight reaction is a natural part of being human. It can even save lives in extreme situations. Small doses of the fight-flight reaction actually help people to enjoy adventure films and the scary rides at amusement parks as their hearts beat a little faster and their bodies perk up. Generally, people find a little adrenaline pleasurable, just as prehistoric humans did when they acted out the day's hunt around a fire.

People usually function well with arousal levels that allow them to stay alert to the normal anxieties about crossing busy streets, lighting gas stoves, and paying bills when they're due. A certain amount of anxiety helps people to foresee negative outcomes and avoid them. People's brains and bodies remain programmed with the fight-flight reaction whether they need such emergency energy or not.

What happens if a stressful work situation or an easily aroused temperament keeps triggering the fight-flight reaction in you? Is it necessary to go along with the prehistoric survival programming, or do employees need to use willpower to suppress the natural fight-flight reaction? Shouldn't these reactions go the way of the dinosaurs and become extinct?

No, the fight-flight reaction *can* help us at work.

ANXIETY REACTION 2: SEPARATION ANXIETY AND FEAR OF STRANGERS

As infants, we rely heavily on others, usually parents, to give us security and comfort—to make us feel safe in an often stressful and confusing world. Because infants focus their feelings of safety on their primary caregivers, they learn, at an early age, to be fearful of strangers, and feel anxious when separated from their parents or caretakers. This anxiety can be expressed by pouting, acting out, or even screaming when separated from parents for a few minutes.

Many psychologists believe that this early separation anxiety, coupled with fear of strangers, establishes the pattern for later fear and anxiety reactions. These early responses create a biological foundation that adults may express in many types of avoidance behavior or as an urge to cling to the safety of the familiar.

BIOLOGY IS ONLY THE BEGINNING

How strongly people initially react to danger or to the unfamiliar may depend on temperament or inherited arousal levels and patterns. Those whose nervous systems are difficult to activate may appear almost fearless, while those who are hyperalert may sense threats and danger even in the safest place.

The first group would be prone to act without any anticipatory anxiety. Because they are unaware of the risks, they tend to suffer negative outcomes more frequently. The second group would be too inhibited to enjoy a sunset, because they would be worried about the possible hazards of the approaching night. What early tribe of humans, or a modern organization, would be complete without a few fearless risk-takers to frighten enemies, try new foods, and find new paths? And what group would be complete

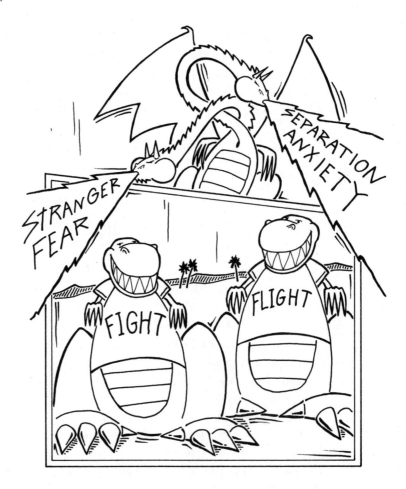

without the restless sleepers who would wake up the entire camp at the first sign of danger?

Most people fall somewhere between these two groups. Many people lean toward the second group and are sometimes too-alert or too-worried. Does your body react with the fight-flight reaction at inopportune times, such as when the boss asks to meet with you about a customer complaint or when a co-worker requests help at quitting time? Because anger and fear reactions are so closely related, do you find yourself responding with irritation or belligerence when you feel anxious? Do you sometimes passively withdraw when your initial feeling was angry frustration or rage? Even when anger is appropriate, sometimes people overreact and end up feeling guilt and even fearing their own hostile reactions.

Long or frequent arousal of the fight-flight reaction can also cause a sort of systems shutdown. People stop responding altogether and lose interest in their jobs, friends, family activities, and usual recreations.

Although individual temperaments and bodily reactions are largely inherited, *biology is only the beginning.* You can learn to actively choose your response to anxiety-provoking situations.

HOW WOULD YOU REACT?

Here are six work situations that usually evoke a fight-flight reaction (Reaction One) or create separation anxiety and fear of strangers (Reaction Two). After reading each scene, see if you can determine which anxiety reaction was triggered.

1.   Ron has been asked by his supervisor, Mr. Rex, to begin using the new computer program that handles the billing for the entire department. He is to begin Monday morning. It means learning new operations and moving to another office away from his two best friends in accounting. Ron is thinking about calling in sick Monday or coming in early to tell Mr. Rex that he isn't ready, even though he knows this is a great career opportunity. ■

Which type of anxiety reaction has been triggered?

Reaction one: Fight-flight   ☐   Reaction two: Separation
                                                          anxiety/fear of strangers   ☐

Has something similar happened to you?

Yes ☐   No ☐

2.   Maria has a new co-worker, Amy, who seems to spend more time at the coffee machine and in the photocopy room than she does at her desk. Amy is always polite and friendly, but lately she's begun to get back late from her lunch breaks as well. Maria hesitates to confront Amy about the neglect of work, even though it means more work for Maria. ■

Which type of anxiety reaction has been triggered?

Reaction one: Fight-flight   ☐   Reaction two: Separation
                                                          anxiety/fear of strangers   ☐

Has something similar happened to you?

Yes ☐   No ☐

3.   Ed manages the personnel department for a large manufacturing firm and gets along well with all his employees. He enjoys speaking with them individually or in small groups of three or four. He gets the jitters, however, whenever he has to address the whole group of 25 in monthly staff meetings. His mouth gets dry, his hands shake, and he gets so dizzy that he's sometimes afraid he'll faint. ■

Which type of anxiety reaction has been triggered?

Reaction one: Fight-flight ☐   Reaction two: Separation
                                       anxiety/fear of strangers ☐

Has something similar happened to you?

Yes ☐   No ☐

4.   Elizabeth absolutely hates the new procedures and the new forms for extending additional credit to customers, especially to those who've been with the company for years. She complains to everyone about the new procedures and bypasses them whenever she can, but refuses to say anything to Mr. Rex about her feelings. Instead, she's become increasingly sarcastic and negative, and Mr. Rex is ready to fire her. Only her many years with the company has stopped him so far. ■

Which type of anxiety reaction has been triggered?

Reaction one: Fight-flight ☐   Reaction two: Separation
                                       anxiety/fear of strangers ☐

Has something similar happened to you?

Yes ☐   No ☐

5.   Fernando is by far InfoWare's top computer software salesperson and everyone loves his bright smile and great sense of humor. When it comes time to do his quar-

terly sales report, he starts calling in to say he'll be late—and then usually calls back later to say he's sick and won't be in at all. He worries that everyone will laugh at his writing, and his reports are always at least a few days late. ■

Which type of anxiety reaction has been triggered?

Reaction one: Fight-flight ☐   Reaction two: Separation anxiety/fear of strangers ☐

Has something similar happened to you?

Yes ☐   No ☐

6.   Amy has recently started on a new high-paying job, but she's afraid that she'll make a mistake that will cost the company a small fortune. Because she has no confidence in her math skills, she restricts herself to light typing, photocopying, and other tasks that keep her away from her accounting responsibilities. She knows it is only a matter of time before her co-workers and Mr. Rex find out, but she doesn't know what to do. ■

Which type of anxiety reaction has been triggered?

Reaction one: Fight-flight ☐   Reaction two: Separation anxiety/fear of strangers ☐

Has something similar happened to you?

Yes ☐   No ☐

Some Solutions

All of these employees allowed anxiety to interfere with their work to some degree. All experienced the disruptive nervous energy of the fight-flight reaction although some showed behavior more closely related to separation anxiety.

Were you able to identify with at least one of these work situations? Then you are on your way to the changes begun by insight. Some possible

2

solutions follow, but remember that insight is more important than a good score. Score one point for each right answer.

1. Here Reaction Two dominates. Ron is clinging to the familiar and fears the unknown. He wants to stay with his friends and is anxious about being separated from the security of his old work routine. Calling in sick is a poor way to deal with the problem. If he can summon the courage to speak with Mr. Rex, he might gain additional confidence to take on this new job opportunity with a little encouragement.

2. Maria is facing the fight-flight dilemma. She is justifiably angry with Amy's mysterious work habits. She must calmly talk to Amy about the burden she is putting on her co-workers. Maybe Amy has some special problem or is not fully aware of her job responsibilities (as shown in example 6). Whatever the reason, Maria must use her fight-flight response to take action. Otherwise, she may wind up ranting at Amy when she's had it with Amy's work avoidance.

3. Reaction one is the cause. Ed faces stage fright with a group of co-workers he knows well. There are really no unknowns or strangers, but his mind and body register a threat and the fight-flight reaction takes over. Anticipatory anxiety during the days or hours before his staff meetings causes him to imagine embarrassing scenes, where he faints or blurts out inappropriate words. He fears the loss of control sometimes experienced by great actors. It hasn't happened yet, but his nervous feelings still persist. He needs to work directly on this fear before he can be comfortable making presentations.

4. Separation anxiety is causing trouble for Elizabeth. She is aggressively clinging to the old ways and old customers. Ironically, her separation anxiety may lead her to be separated from a job she's had for years. Her only hope is to put her newfound energy to good use: speak candidly, but respectfully, with Mr. Rex about some modifications of the new procedures.

5. Fernando seems confident when confronting people and taking on challenges. However, he clings to familiar patterns and rejects his need to work on his writing skills, which seem foreign and strange to him. The late reports and calling in late and sick are unusual compared to his usual world-beating attitude and accomplishments. In fact, he experiences separation anxiety when asked to learn something new.

6. Amy is besieged by both the types of anxiety. She clings to the skills she knows, and she's afraid to confront her co-worker, Maria, or Mr. Rex, with the truth. Sooner or later, her lateness and avoidance of accounting will get her into trouble, and perhaps fired. She can avoid

these negative outcomes by admitting to Maria or another co-worker that she needs help, or by getting lessons outside the office.

Now That You Know the Score

Neither the human reactions developed in prehistory nor the reactions you developed in your infancy should completely determine your responses in the workplace. These two main sources of nervous energy are universal biological reactions to danger. As illustrated in the work situations, how we deal with these reactions—how we respond to our reactions—still remains our responsibility as adults, no matter how automatic or intense our reactions may be. With some training and some courage, you can modify your reactions and even put them to good use at work. For now, it is your score that counts.

- If you scored less than three points, review this chapter before going on.
- If you scored at least three points, then you understand the anxiety reactions.

Chapter Checkpoints

✓ Fight-flight reactions are as old as the human race.

✓ Separation anxiety and fear of strangers are usually developed during infancy.

✓ Anxious energy can be tamed and redirected for job advancement.

3

Tranquility through Feedback

This chapter will help you to:

- Practice calming down.
- Train for the Anxiety Olympics.
- Begin to apply anti-anxiety techniques at work.

This is an action chapter, where you'll learn to take physical action toward addressing anxiety. As you now realize, your body reacts to perceptions of danger in physical expressions of anxiety. It's time to disrupt those patterns physically.

NEGATIVE FEEDBACK PATTERNS

From the Chapter 1 inventory, you should have a clear idea of how your body reacts to anxiety-provoking situations at work. Although it's possible to suffer from only one or two forms of physical discomfort brought on by anxious feelings, your body probably reacts with all or almost all the typical signs at one time or another. These signs include rapid pulse and breathing, profuse sweating, stomach problems, swallowing or speaking difficulties, giddiness, headaches, trembling, and blurred vision.

A little nervous system arousal makes people feel alert and alive—a little edge that can make people more productive. Too much arousal, however, can be distressing and even painful. A pounding heart can sometimes panic people into believing that they are seconds away from cardiac arrest. How many times have you used or heard the expression, "I thought I'd have a heart attack!"

Bodies generally react to a frightening situation with fight-flight energy mobilization. People feel and notice the discomfort (making them more fearful), and then their bodies react even more strongly, sometimes piling on new discomforts. Caught in such a negative feedback loop, people have difficulty acting rationally and become ineffective. You can physically train yourself to break the pattern.

TRAINING FOR THE ANXIETY OLYMPICS

Athletes don't learn the rules and techniques of competition during their contests. They train and strengthen their bodies through repetitive exercises of the routine maneuvers of their sport.

In the competition, contests, and team play of the workplace, people are constantly giving good advice when they say, "Calm down." How many people actually know how to calm down and relax in tense situations, when a shipment is lost, the computer system goes down, or they are accused of botching a great opportunity? Even those people who are natu-

rally or temperamentally low-key do not seem able to calm down in such stressful situations. Why? They don't practice enough. Few people have taken the time to practice this Olympic feat before the trials and main events of work.

You're Getting Sleepier and Sleepier: Feedback Training

A good training model for relaxing and calming down is sleep. Breathing is slow and deep, heart rate and blood pressure drop, and muscles lose most of their tension. Going to sleep is an early response to stress, and most people know that a good night's rest can renew the body and mind, reset energy levels, and brighten spirits significantly. However, chronic sleep disorders can severely impair a person's ability to work and may require medical treatment.

Except for firefighters and certain types of medical personnel on call, sleeping on the job will lead to trouble, so be careful when training at work. Most training should be done in a classroom setting, at home, or during lunch breaks. If you're distracted by people and noise, find an isolated and quiet place. Start thinking as an Olympic athlete training and practicing for the Anxiety Hurdles.

Warning: Program One and Program Two must be practiced every day for at least two weeks before significant results appear. Even though some people respond after only a few days, most participants will need steady training for two weeks to combat years of negative feedback patterns. Schedule 15 to 20 minutes every day (at a definite time) to train. Make it a rule and force yourself to follow through. Use the Anxiety Date Book after the Post-Test to keep track of your progress.

Steps	Program One
Step one	Sleep—make sure you're getting enough. Too little sleep may make you jittery and nervous, maintaining a higher state of arousal than needed. You must be rested enough to resist actually falling asleep while training. Experiment with more sleep at night or try taking short catnaps. Athletes need a store of calm energy and so do you.
Step two	Sit—get comfortable and let your muscles relax. If necessary, progressively tense and then relax parts of your body in turn.
Step three	Close your eyes—let yourself sink into the darkness without falling asleep. Imagine a pleasant, tranquil scene such as a picnic spot near a lake.
Step four	Breathe slowly—fill your lungs with air and exhale as though you were lightly blowing out birthday candles. Find a comfortable rhythm.

Steps	Program One
Step five	Find the feeling—continue steps two, three, and four until you've captured a clear feeling of calm and relaxation.
Step six	Name the feeling—identify the feeling with a word, image, color, sound—anything that helps summon this sense of relaxation.

Mark your anxiety date book.

Practice steps two, three, four, and five for approximately 15 minutes a day. Try step six on the third or fourth session, but don't worry if a name or image doesn't stick. Your brain and body will eventually pick one for you. Step 5 may be difficult for some to achieve. If you have trouble, spend more time on each session or try two sessions a day. Don't give up. Everybody can learn to relax. Some employees find it easier to relax if they repeat phrases such as "I feel myself getting calmer and more relaxed." Once you've mastered steps two through five, begin Program Two.

Steps	Program Two
Step one	Open your eyes—starting from step five of Program One, slowly lift your eyelids without looking at anything in particular. Maintain your calm feeling. If it starts to fade, try closing your eyes halfway until you get it back again.
Step two	Look around—while keeping your sense of relaxation, take note of your surroundings in a superficial, impressionistic way. Keep the feeling of calm; if it begins to subside, close your eyes and return to step one.
Step three	Slowly stand—or change to a more alert position, if you cannot stand, while maintaining the calm feeling. Sit down, if the feeling begins to fade.
Step four	Walk or move—slowly move a few feet away. Keep your sense of calm. Return to earlier steps, if necessary.
Step five	Recite—begin reciting your name, telephone number, address, and any other well-known information as you move. Maintain the sense of relaxation.
Step six	Exercise—stop reciting and do any easy light exercise that increases heart rate and speeds up breathing. Avoid exercises that cause too much discomfort. Try to maintain your basic calm feeling for a few minutes even though your body is working harder. Return to earlier steps when necessary.

Mark your anxiety date book.

Don't be discouraged by the difficulties of Program Two. It may take more than one session to progress to another step, since the steps get harder. If you think of Program One as limbering-up exercises, then Program Two is weight training.

You may need to spend several sessions alone on achieving step six, especially if you're not used to exercising. (If you hate exercising, just put your arms straight out in front of you. Spread them wide, and close them again. Then lift them straight over your head. Repeat.)

You don't need to master Program Two to go on to Program Three. Be sure that you've tried all the steps in Program Two at least two or three times. Since it may take weeks to complete Programs One and Two, move on to Chapter 4 while still continuing to practice your anxiety feedback training—perhaps even before you attempt Program Three.

3

However, it is vital that you work on Program Three as soon as you've completed Program Two—or at least attempted its steps a few times.

Steps	Program Three
Step one	Invite the feeling—during the normal course of your work day (while sorting the mail, checking your messages, or performing some simple task) try using the word *calm,* or the image, sound, or color developed in Step six of Program One to bring on your feeling of calm and relaxation. Gradually, extend this exercise to other activities—without losing the sense of calm and without losing your concentration on the task. In normal conversations at home and at work, also start inviting your sense of calm.
Step two	Combine the two sixes—while doing your Program Two, Step six, light exercise (or while walking vigorously to work) use the word *calm* or your image from Step six in Program One to help bring on your relaxed, calm feeling.
Step three	Pick a fight—start a little friendly spat or teasing dispute with a friend or family member. Pretend you are angry, raise your voice, and complain dramatically about something. At the same time, try to keep your calm feeling. Be careful: don't pick on anyone sensitive or with a poor sense of humor; make sure your mock fight doesn't escalate into a real argument. Keep the subject silly enough to be obvious. Skip this step if you can't find a safe subject or person with whom to play fight.
Step four	Put yourself in "danger"—deliberately put yourself in a situation that makes you feel very slightly anxious. Practice bringing on your calm feeling. Try this several times. Whether you succeed or not, move on to another anxiety-provoking situation. Remember you are training, only sparring with your fears. Don't try anything too fear-provoking or dangerous. Keep it light.
Step five	Keep your cool (calm)—try bringing on your relaxation and sense of calm in a mildly anxiety-provoking situation that spontaneously happens at work. Try it on at least three separate occasions before returning to earlier steps. Don't attempt to use your calm feeling on more difficult situations until you've mastered at least three or four mildly anxiety-provoking ones. Build up slowly.
Step six	Heavy duty workouts—with several successes at Step five under your belt, try invoking your sense of calm in the most anxiety-producing situations for you at work. Perhaps you've been avoiding routine tasks, greater responsibilities, or opportunities because of the discomfort that your anxiety brings. Try using your calm feeling against the pains of these situations. Although your relief from these discomforts may be little at first, gradually your tolerance to the anxiety will increase.

Mark your anxiety date book at the end of the book. Don't get discouraged. It may take months to achieve Steps four, five, and six.

What's Next?

Feedback training is often an effective physical approach to reducing your anxiety. Some people can learn to calm themselves with feedback training alone. Most people need to combine feedback training with other techniques. We'll cover these throughout the book.

Chapter Checkpoints

✓ Dealing calmly with anxiety takes training and practice.

✓ Daily training builds calming abilities.

✓ Gradually extend the calm feeling into more work situations to push anxiety away.

✓ Just as weight lifters build stamina, taking more risks builds tolerance to feelings of anxiety.

CHAPTER

4 | Self-Knowledge Reduces Anxiety

This chapter will help you to:

- Develop your own personality profile.
- Target characteristics you'd like to change.
- Work toward a better fit between you and your co-workers.

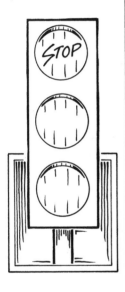

One cause of stress and anxiety at work is the common tension that arises when many different personalities bump up against each other. We've all seen what happens when normally pleasant and agreeable individuals find themselves in constant conflict with each other due to marked differences in temperament and point of view. Everyone feels the steady buildup of anxiety and friction that eventually erupts into confrontation.

A way to nip these tensions in the bud is to first assess your *actual* characteristics at work, then create a picture of your *ideal* characteristics at work. By comparing your actual self with your ideal self, you'll target behaviors you want to change. Changing some behaviors could lead to smoothing daily interactions with your co-workers, and thereby reduce anxiety.

IT'S YOUR TURN

How do you see yourself at work? One way to get a quick reading is to work with a small deck of cards with descriptive words written on them. On pp. 97-105, there are 30 words inside numbered boxes that can be cut out and made into cards. Either cut these boxes out or copy each number and word onto a blank card (almost any size index card will work fine). You'll have 30 cards, each with a number and a descriptive word on one side. The other side should remain blank.

Once the 30 cards are ready, begin to sort them.

Make a pile of those cards that describe you at work, a *like* pile (for characteristics you see in yourself). At the same time, make a separate *unlike* pile for cards that don't describe you at work (for characteristics you don't see in yourself). Once you have the two piles, put them in order. The top card in your *like* pile should be the word that best describes you at work. Then put the card with the word that describes you second best directly under the top card, and so on.

Now, beginning with the top card, write the card numbers and words in the order you ranked them in the following table (include today's date). Make copies of the blank *like*, *unlike*, and *ideal* tables to repeat the exercise at a later date.

Like at Work

Card Number Top Card = 1	Word	Date

Card Number Top Card = 1	Word	Date

Unlike at Work

Take the *unlike* pile and rank the cards with the card least like you on top, followed by the next least like you, and so on. Write the date and the card numbers and words, starting with the top card just as you did for the *like* pile.

Card Number Top Card = 1	Word	Date

Card Number Top Card = 1	Word	Date

Stacking the Deck in Your Favor

Who do you want to be at work? Look carefully through the *unlike* pile and pull out those cards that you wish applied to you at work. Then go through the *like* pile and pick the cards that are the most favorable or those that you wish described you more strongly. Now rank this new *ideal* pile and write them below just as you did with the like and unlike piles.

Ideal at Work

Card Number Top Card = 1	Word	Date

Card Number Top Card = 1	Word	Date

4

Compare your *like* pile with your *ideal* pile at work, to find whole areas to target for improvement. Note the unfavorable words in your *like* pile as well. Suppose *helpful* was not in the *like* pile, but it's in the *ideal* pile at work. How could you become more helpful to other employees? Would you need to learn more about other people's jobs, or would an attitude change be enough? If you consider *shy* one of the unfavorable words in your *like* pile, what steps can you take to act outgoing with your fellow workers?

Take Action

Taking steps toward becoming the person you describe in your *ideal* pile may be frightening at first, but any changes you make toward your ideal self will actually increase your confidence and lower your anxiety. Circle the words in your *ideal* list that already describe you at least to some extent. Put check marks next to those traits that you know you can gain with a little work. Draw double exclamation points next to those words that will take extra work to become true. See how many words you can change from checks to circles and from exclamation points to checks as you work through this book.

Cards at Home

You'll be using these cards later, so keep them. Right now make *like* and *unlike* piles to describe yourself at home. Compare the cards in your at home piles to those in your at work piles. Are you closer to your *ideal* pile at work with your *like* pile at home? If so, maybe you can transplant some of your at home self to work.

If possible, have a co-worker and someone at home sort a pile for you, a like pile and unlike pile. Compare the way they see you with the way you see yourself. Is it better or worse? Do you need to communicate more about yourself?

Future Sorts

Periodically, without looking at previous sorts, use the cards again to get a reading on yourself. After you have your piles separated and the rank orders written down, compare them to the previous ones. Keep them dated and note any improvements. You may want to add cards with new words. Just be sure to keep the same number of positive and negative words.

Chapter Checkpoints

✓ Taking an inventory of your positive and negative characteristics will give you target areas to improve.

✓ Imagining an ideal work self provides a goal for real changes.

✓ Self-knowledge of your work self can lead to better teamwork on the job.

5 | Self-Confidence Reduces Anxiety

This chapter will help you to:

- Discover your basic pattern of expectations.
- Learn the benefits of risk-taking, courage, and imagination.
- Find out how to manage risks.

This is an insight chapter. Finding patterns in your anxiety can lead to confidence. Explore the ideas here to reduce anxiety and gain a greater feeling of confidence. Follow directions carefully, and work through each exercise. Ask yourself: How can the insights gained through each exercise be applied to my job performance?

A PICTURE WORTH LESS THAN 200 WORDS

Look carefully at the following drawing of the trapeze artists. Imagine what led up to this scene and write about it here or on a separate sheet of paper.

Part One. What Led up to This Scene?

_____
_____
_____
_____
_____
_____
_____
_____
_____

Write how the story in the picture ends or what the next picture in this scene might look like. Describe how the characters think and feel.

5

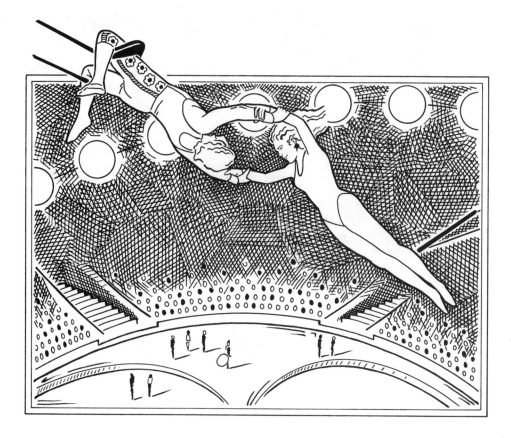

Part Two. How Does the Story in the Picture End?

_____

_____

_____

_____

_____

_____

By writing Parts One and Two, you have created a mini-story based on a similar circus scene used extensively in research on expectations (R. May 1980).

Now read through what you wrote for Part One. Was your description positive (showing satisfaction, pleasure, confidence, or achievement) or negative (showing worry, conflict, tension, or failure)? Do the same for Part Two.

| Part One | Positive ☐ | or | Negative ☐ |
| Part Two | Positive ☐ | or | Negative ☐ |

Most stories for this picture change from Part One to Part Two—from positive to negative or from negative to positive. If you checked two positives or two negatives, look at your descriptions again. Did you use words that involve physical injury, discomfort, or risk; poverty or intense need; doubt or lack of awareness? Using words that give any impression of a negative feeling or situation should be judged a negative evaluation of Part One or Part Two. Words that give the impression of growth, strength, mutual affection or concern would be scored as positive.

Reevaluate Parts One and Two. If you changed your original story, or thought of something else first, write down your earliest response. The natural break between Part One and Part Two may have been made too early or too late. If necessary, transfer some sentences from one Part to another.

Most likely you now have a positive-negative or negative-positive pattern for Parts One and Two. (If you still have a positive-positive or negative-negative pattern, it is ok, as you'll see below.) If there is such a contrast, your story follows one of two basic patterns. One pattern is rags-to-riches, going from low status to high (as seen in the stories of *Rocky*, Cinderella, *Working Girl*, or President Lincoln). The other pattern is tragedy, with a fall from the heights (such as General Custer, Julius Caesar, or Prometheus). The negative-positive pattern is the typical American success story and the positive-negative is the Greek tragedy misfortune.

Negative to Positive

If part one of your mini-story is strongly negative, you may feel like an underdog in competitive situations, perhaps too aware of the forces working against your efforts for success. You may be too passive, hoping that good luck or opportunities will come your way. You probably tend to wait to be offered promotions or more responsibility. This rarely happens except in fast-growing or high-turnover industries. Your ambitions have not yet gone beyond the daydreaming stage.

Your basic belief in happy endings or ultimate triumph is definitely favorable, but your attitude toward achieving your goals may be too passive. No one will know that you really want to take on more responsibilities if you don't openly communicate your desire in a meeting with a supervisor. Don't wait to be discovered.

Positive to Negative

You are, at least on the surface, confident about your ability to be competitive at work, with a fairly good idea of the risks involved. If your mini-story went from being positive ("they're the top act in the circus" or "the team is perfect") to strongly negative ("she dies" or "he drops her and there's no net"), then insecurities concerning your abilities and fear of failure lie just beneath the surface. You may feel overshadowed in your efforts at work. You may believe that you can't measure up no matter what you achieve. Milder contrasts might merely reflect a true appreciation of the difficulties involved in getting ahead and/or that you have had some direct experience with failure. Don't let imagined failures stop you.

Positive-Positive

You tend to act confidently in many job-related areas, and you expect to ultimately succeed. Although you are ambitious, you may not be fully aware of the risks involved or the level of competition for positions or money. On the surface, you may feel prepared to handle new responsibilities, but wishing for a happy ending may not be enough. Make sure that confidence is backed up by skill and not bravado. Back up your confidence with real commitment.

Negative-Negative

Are you depressed or just having a bad day? If you have just experienced a serious loss or disappointment (or series of losses), then your mini-story reflects your feelings about recent events. If negative-negative is typical of your outlook, then you may need to make some big changes before you find satisfaction.

This kind of story may indicate low self-esteem and full awareness of the risk of failure. You expect the future to be as bad (or even worse) than the past and present. Work on improving your confidence and skills.

YOU BET YOUR LIFE

Feelings of fear or anxiety alert people to the risks of living. Without such strong warnings, people would be in constant danger of trouble, injury, or death.

Since it's impossible to play it completely safe and still get the things that will bring satisfaction, people *must* take some risks. In other words: People must deliberately put themselves in danger or at risk.

On a daily basis, everyone takes risks to secure positive results. Skeptical? Check the risks you take in the following list:

Risk	Make a Check or Leave Blank
Traveling by car, truck, or motorcycle.	☐
Traveling by bus or trolley.	☐
Traveling by train or subway.	☐
Traveling by plane, ship, or ferry.	☐
Riding a horse, bike, or walking.	☐
Walking up or down a flight of stairs.	☐
Smoking or living in a large city.	☐
Working outdoors.	☐
Working around machinery.	☐
Using electricity or gas.	☐
Driving without an airbag or seatbelt.	☐
Being overweight or underweight.	☐
Postponing medical checkups or care.	☐

This list could go on indefinitely. If you checked even one, you have been taking risks. Every one of these risks could lead to serious illness or injury, possibly resulting in death. People take these, and other risks, in order to achieve desired results and goals.

RISK, COURAGE, AND EXPECTATION

When in situations where loss, disappointment, or even injury and death are possible, people usually feel anxiety. Fearlessness might sometimes be perceived as insensitivity, stupidity, or thoughtlessness, but it should never be confused with courage. Courage is acting appropriately even though you feel fearful. Courage usually comes only with education. People must learn to act bravely.

Since the days of taking risks as toddlers, people were encouraged or discouraged by their caretakers. Usually by age 10 or 12, people learn to calculate most risks fairly well, given enough information. What if the information is wrong or inadequate? Expectations of loss and gain could easily cause someone to plunge into danger unnecessarily, or be overcome with needless fear.

ANTICIPATORY ANXIETY: FEAR OF RISKS

Using imagination to solve simple, everyday problems at home and work, and to anticipate losses and gains is so natural that people are hardly aware of their reliance on this talent.

People employ their imaginations so frequently that they have become powerful tools—so powerful that people's bodies may react as though an imagined situation were actually happening. People can be swept away on waves of emotion just by imagining some magnificent gain or some devastating loss.

When people react to danger with the fight-flight response, they feel fear or anger. However, when they react with fear to an imagined or anticipated danger it's called *anticipatory anxiety,* which can become a problem in itself.

The discomfort of anticipatory anxiety persuades you that it is *bad* to volunteer for new assignments, *dangerous* to request better job benefits, and *reckless* to transfer to a new department. You feel the risk is too great and choose instead to avoid bodily discomfort based on a preliminary use of your vivid imagination. However, you can learn to control your own imagination by managing risks.

RISK MANAGEMENT MODELS

Most automobile drivers have learned to accept the risks involved with driving, because they depend so much on this means of transportation. People choose to drive without wearing seatbelts. People assert their independence and boast about their driving skills. Whether they are or not, they feel in control—right up to the moment they're almost sideswiped by a bus or truck. The rush of adrenaline reminds them that more than pride is at stake.

Basically, people have determined that the benefits of driving outweigh the risks because of two main reasons. One is that the driver is directly (if only partially) controlling the risk. The other is that driving or riding in cars is so familiar that the risks seem normal and natural. It's nothing to get excited about. People learn not to react with too much anxiety (Konner 1990).

5

Being an airline passenger is different. Usually, the pilot doesn't let you have a turn at the throttle, especially during takeoffs and landings. You are helpless to influence the process. The fact is, you are helpless to manage the risks.

Smokers handle taking high risks concerning heart disease and cancer in two additional ways. First, they learn to delay any concern because their potential losses due to smoking are remote—sometimes 20 or 30 years away. Second, they are able to frame the risk philosophically or conveniently: "You've got to die of something." Or, "I don't want to gain weight because that's dangerous, too."

Although these are extreme cases, they provide some clues about managing potentially less dangerous risks and possible losses.

Guide for Questionable Risk-Taking

As you pursue your career and practice Steps four, five, and six of Program Three found in Chapter 3, ask yourself these questions about any risk you plan to take.

1. What do I have to lose? Determining the potential losses in any situation is always the first step in any risky business.

2. What do I gain if taking these risks pays off? How good are the rewards? Do they outweigh the possible losses?

3. Am I concentrating too much on the worst case possibility? Many employees and managers believe that if they've provided for the worst possible results, then they needn't worry. Or they panic because they can't stop thinking that a catastrophe will strike.

4. Have I spent most of my energy on likely outcomes? Learn to prepare mentally and physically for the most common and likely outcomes of your actions, good as well as bad (Lewis 1980).

5. Can I reframe the risks involved more accurately in philosophical terms or more conveniently in practical terms? "Okay, if Ms. Blanco turns me down for a raise, she'll be providing me with a good reason to push for a transfer to the personnel department." Or, "If I find myself in trouble working on the new assignment, I'll ask Mukta to help me after work."

6. Am I risking only discomfort or embarrassment? In unfamiliar or difficult situations, everyone feels discomfort or suffers embarrassment. Slowly build up tolerance to these painful sensations and remind yourself that in the end, it doesn't really matter.

Chapter Checkpoints

✓ People tend to expect success and/or failure in a certain pattern: positive-positive, positive-negative, negative-positive, or negative-negative.

✓ Anticipatory anxiety—imagining a negative result—can sometimes become the problem.

Ask six questions before taking any risk:

1. What do I have to lose?
2. What do I gain if my risk-taking pays off?
3. Am I concentrating too much on the worst case possibility?
4. Have I spent most of my energy on likely outcomes?
5. Can I reframe the risks involved more accurately or more practically?
6. Am I risking only discomfort or embarrassment?

CHAPTER

6

Reduce Anxiety by Facing It

This chapter will help you to:

- Directly combat your anxiety reactions.
- Build psychological muscles.
- Analyze your anxiety to create an ongoing action plan.

On his second throw into the sea, the poor fisherman dragged back a strange bottle in his net. Still no fish for his hungry family. In frustration he pulled the cork and watched in amazement as a surge of purple smoke from the bottle formed a hundred-foot tall blue genie that towered over him and blocked out the sun. ''Prepare for thy doom!'' boomed the genie's terrible voice. ''Wait!'' yelled the fisherman. ''Why am I doomed?'' The genie raged horribly, ''In the first thousand years of my captivity, I vowed to make my liberator rich beyond dreams, but I was not freed. In the second thousand years, I pledged to make whosoever uncorked me from that evil bottle the ruler of all earthly kingdoms, but in the last five thousand years, I swore that I would kill the first mortal I laid eyes upon.'' Though terrified, the fisherman began to laugh. ''You dare to laugh?!'' ranted the genie. ''Because you are joking,'' replied the fisherman between chuckles. ''Surely, a genie of your size does not have the power to fit into this small container.'' Roaring, ''I will prove it!'' the genie dissolved into smoke and whisked into the bottle. Quickly, the fisherman plugged in the cork and threw the bottle into the sea. The next cast of his net returned a hundred fish, and both he and his family were saved. ■

PROFILES IN COURAGE

This is an action chapter. Change only becomes real when you do something. Talk to people who've performed heroic acts, who've risked their lives in war, or who've acted to save other lives during disasters. Were they

afraid? Absolutely, but they did not spend too much time thinking about their fear. Instead, they put all their energy into acting quickly. Their overwhelming need to act pushed them to confront the danger directly. Few intended to act bravely; their circumstances seemed to demand their courageous actions.

Stories like "The Fisherman and the Genie" demonstrate how circumstantial courage works. Suddenly, you are thrust into a frightening or unknown situation, and only acting with courage and swift insight can save the day. Folktales, legends, and myths try to teach this lesson: Use the energy from the fear to act against the fear—have faith in yourself to find the solutions your imagination will create.

PARADOXICAL PRESCRIPTION

Viktor Frankl, a psychoanalyst and the inventor of Logotherapy, discovered that if people stop using energy to fight their fears, but learn to laugh at them instead, the anxiety reactions gradually go away just like the genie in the story. He calls this technique of humorously concentrating on and exaggerating reactions *paradoxical intention* (Frankl 1986).

Suppose you sweat under stress. Perspiration pours from your brow into your eyes, and your hands shake like leaves. You have to meet and convince a government official to give your company an important contract. Do you insist on talking to him outside in the cold, so your shaking and sweating won't be noticeable? No, follow Dr. Frankl's advice.

Try playing with the fear. Make fun of yourself. Say to yourself, "Okay, there's Mr. Federal Grant. I need to sweat and shake just as much as I can, more than ever. I'm going to try for a record today." Joke and laugh about your fear. Tease your anxiety reactions; try to make them worse. Don't suppress those tremors—exaggerate them. Just refuse to take them seriously.

Interfering with the Interference

Anticipatory anxiety clearly comes into play when people worry about their job performance. People worry about anxiety reactions: "I'm afraid I'm going to shake like a leaf when we meet with the new clients." Naturally, anticipation of the anxiety reaction usually causes it to happen (in this case, shaking).

Suppose you have to make a presentation before an audience of 300 other employees, explaining some new medical benefits. You're terrified that your mind will go blank. Your anticipatory anxiety about your mind going blank may make you lose your train of thought. Even with notes and other preparations, your worry will more than likely interfere with your performance. The solution is to interfere with the interference.

Tell your audience that although you have all the facts in your head and written on the papers in front of your, your mind may go blank. Make it a joke. "My mind may go blank at any time, so watch out." Actually pretend at some point in your presentation that your mind has gone blank, and then say, "Only kidding." Teasing an anxiety reaction in this way interferes with it, but it takes practice.

Building Psychological Muscles

On the lines below, describe three at work situations that usually cause some simple anxiety reactions, such as rapid breathing, choking sensation, or a facial tic. Next to the situation, note your usual anxiety reaction. Look back at the Physical Inventory of Chapter 1 and the Self-Assessment if necessary.

At Work Situation	Anxiety Reaction
1. _____	_____
_____	_____
2. _____	_____
_____	_____
3. _____	_____
_____	_____

6

To supplement the physical training from Chapter 3, practice exaggerating and making fun of anxiety reactions according to Dr. Frankl's paradoxical prescription. Of the three at work situations you've written above, pick the one that causes the least fear and whose anxiety reactions are the easiest to exaggerate. Then follow these steps below:

Step one	Outside of the at work situation, try to produce the anxiety reaction. Exaggerate it, talk to it (or yourself), and tease it. Use your imagination to bring on the feeling. "Okay, Jose, let's get that voice quivering. Voice, you're much too steady; let's get going."
Step two	Look at the anxiety reaction with humor: In effect, create a comedy routine relevant to the situation. "So, you're going to faint? Well, faint right here on the street. Don't wait until you get to work. You can call and explain from the hospital later if you're not run over by a car."
Step three	After practicing outside of work, use your routine in the situation that usually provokes the anxiety reaction. Do not suppress the reaction. Deliberately try to make it appear. "Oh, oh, there's the vice president for sales. Now, I have to choke up as much as I can when I tell him this week's figures. Then, he'll really think I'm crazy. Come on, throat, you can do it."

Develop a funny routine for each of the three at work situations that you wrote above. Try each one in turn. See what works, but don't give up. Expand the interfering with the interference to other at work situations you've been avoiding.

BREAKING UP ISN'T HARD TO DO

As you've been reading this book and doing the exercises, you have been analyzing your behavior and anxiety reactions. Examining anxiety in such an objective way helps develop a nonanxious perspective. As you break up anxiety reactions into different parts, you can become more comfortable with the whole idea of your fears. You can become more detached and desensitized to the discomforts that the fight-flight reaction causes.

Combined with the physical training of Chapter 3, your tolerance to the pain of anxiety (both mental and physical) should gradually increase, but only if you keep pushing yourself.

Breaking up anxiety into its parts and examining them under the microscope of the Inventory-Insight-Action process slowly destroys the anxiety's power. Even if it doesn't completely disappear, it becomes manageable.

6

Become an Anxiety Analyst

As we've seen throughout this book, taking inventory, or analyzing a situation, is the first step toward action and change. It's now time to take an even closer look at your anxieties.

You want to know how your anxiety reactions work and what stops the reactions. By writing down times, dates, reactions, and the factors involved, you will become an expert on your own anxiety. Soon you will develop theories about your anxiety and design experiments to test them.

Keep an anxiety journal. Try keeping a daily or weekly anxiety journal of your confrontations with at work anxiety reactions. Include feelings, thoughts, and bodily reactions. Write down whatever seems relevant. Wait at least two weeks before reading what you wrote and then look for patterns and opportunities to initiate more changes.

1. Billions and Billions

Develop a cosmic perspective on your anxieties. Consider all the people on the Earth past and present (about 85 billion). How significant is your particular worry or your particular anxiety reaction? What difference will it make in a thousand years? Or even five years from now? How big are your worries on this scale?

2. Keep Laughing

Laugh. Laugh more. Go to a comedy club. Rent comedy videos. Read Mark Twain.

Some experts believe that laughing is an interrupted cry of fear. Instead of a surprise scaring someone, it becomes fun. In any case, it's hard to be afraid or sad if you're laughing.

If you can, try telling jokes with your co-workers. Maybe your boss has a sense of humor. If so, try to tickle his or her funny bone. Change the tone of work a little if it gets too tense and serious.

With your friends and close co-workers, joke about your at work fears. Exaggerate and act out fearful situations. Be dramatic and try to make them laugh. Remember that the comedians that have become famous telling stories of their fearfulness really were afraid, but through exaggeration and a sense of fun they have developed enough courage to speak before large audiences.

Chapter Checkpoints

✓ Use anxious energy against fear.

✓ Making fun of fears interferes with their effects.

✓ Analyzing anxiety gradually reduces its power.

✓ Laughter is the best antidote for anxiety.

7 | Rating Job Anxieties

This chapter will help you to:

- Rate the stress and anxiety level of your job.
- Understand the relationships among stress, nervous energy, and anxiety.

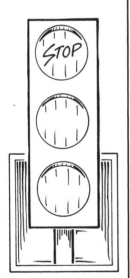

WHAT SCARES ME THE MOST?

What are the things that could happen at work that would turn your blood into ice water? Is getting reprimanded in front of everyone for something you've done your worst fear? Or is it whether or not you'll be fired or demoted?

Rate the work situations below in terms of the fear they create. Use a scale of 0 to 100, but also consider how often you feel afraid. If you are afraid to be fired, but you rarely feel afraid because your performance is so good, rate getting fired low, about 10 or 20. If you often feel afraid that you'll get fired even though you know it's almost impossible, rate getting fired high, perhaps 80 or 90. Some situations may have the same ratings.

At Work Situation	Your Rating
	Scale 0 to 100
Private reprimand by your supervisor.	_____
Public reprimand by your supervisor.	_____
Having to reprimand someone else.	_____
Conflict with co-worker.	_____
Conflict with supervisor.	_____

At Work Situation	Your Rating
	Scale 0 to 100
Mild criticism by co-worker.	_____
Mild criticism by supervisor.	_____
Making slight errors.	_____
Making serious errors.	_____
Getting laid off or fired.	_____
Dealing with customer or client complaints.	_____
Complaints from other departments.	_____
Not meeting deadlines.	_____
Forgetting important tasks or meetings.	_____
Scheduling meetings.	_____
Conducting meetings.	_____
Producing important reports.	_____
Making presentations.	_____
Arriving late.	_____
Being the subject of gossip.	_____
Being sexually harassed.	_____
Being absent.	_____
Asking for a promotion or raise.	_____
Being transferred.	_____

Look at the at work situations on which you scored 50 or above. Some may be the same or similar to the anxiety provoking items you checked earlier in the book. A few may be new. It is clear that fight-flight reactions or separation anxiety and fear of the unknown are present in these high-scored situations.

You may never need to deal with some of these problems, and others may not happen for some time, but the techniques you learn to apply to one set of circumstances can usually be used again in a new context.

Although you may be working on other anxiety reactions and situations, don't forget to add any new at work situations to your agenda. Bring the ammunition you've gathered from Chapters 3 and 6 in a well-planned attack on these problems. Delay a little, if you need to, but remember: To stop being a victim, you must attack.

PRESSURE!

The work world certainly has its own pressures, which people must combat with their own energy. There are deadlines to meet, rush orders to fill, government regulations to follow, documents to prepare or type, mass mailings to be made—a thousand different pressures.

Without some pressure and stress, people's jobs might become dull and meaningless. Without some challenge, employees might become listless and depressed or their spare energy might spill over into worry or destructive behaviors.

Most people, however, are usually overstimulated and overstressed. The message people's brains get is: Produce more energy, faster! But, the faster the pace, the more difficult it is to keep up, and the greater people's nervous systems are energized. They have too much nervous energy.

PRESSURE BECOMES ANXIETY

7

Imagine that it's your job to prepare the thirty 50-page packets for tomorrow's board meeting. Two charts have to be redone completely. Pages 17, 18, and 27 have serious errors that need to be corrected. All the copy machines are out of order except the one in marketing, whose department head is currently warring with your supervisor. It's 4:30 P.M. The meeting is scheduled for 8 A.M. the next day. How do you feel? Perhaps a little pressured? A little anxious? Ready to explode?

How does your body feel—like you want to run? Nervous energy is probably pouring out of you. You're fidgeting, biting your nails, eating everything in sight, playing with your hair, or drinking cup after cup of coffee, but nothing satisfies your need to do something. You're nervous, and your anxiety is growing.

Researchers have found that people operating under strict schedules or in situations of uncertainty, get overstimulated and need to engage in these side behaviors (eating or fidgeting) to maintain their concentration. These side behaviors act like safety valves letting off excess steam—but they may not be enough. Nervous energy easily becomes anxiety, because most side behaviors can't counteract the buildup of pressure, stress, and tension.

How Stressed Are You?

Use the stress list below to determine how much stress you deal with on the job. Check those items that apply to you at work.

Stress List

1. I often feel overworked. ☐
2. My work follows strict schedules. ☐
3. My performance is carefully monitored. ☐
4. Mistakes can cause big problems. ☐
5. I have little choice in my assignments. ☐
6. I can be blamed if something goes wrong. ☐
7. My job involves periodic busy times. ☐
8. I'm often expected to make do without enough help. ☐
9. My supervisors think nothing of adding extra duties. ☐
10. I'm expected to work overtime whenever needed. ☐

Total number checked: ___

If you checked two items or less, you probably don't have too much spillover anxiety (although some days or weeks may be worse than others).

Three to five items checked means that your stress is usually fairly high. There's definitely a danger that stress on the job is adding to your anxious feelings (and perhaps adding to problems at home).

If you've checked more than five items, you are in a high-stress job. With the amount of pressure you have to deal with, it's urgent that you find ways to get relief. Besides anxiety, you are in danger of early heart attacks and other stress-related illnesses. High stress may really be preanxiety.

Even people with low stress may find nervous energy from job-related stress interfering with their job performance. Use the many techniques in this book to relieve your mental and physical stress, dissipate nervous energy, and fend off anxiety.

Chapter Checkpoints

✓ High-rated anxiety situations must be faced and attacked.

✓ Some stress keeps jobs from getting dull.

✓ Too many stressful factors at work can be hazardous to your health.

✓ Nervous energy can spill over into anxiety.

8 | Putting Anxiety in Perspective

This chapter will help you to:

- Learn to mentally jump into danger.
- Rehearse for horrors—and then for success.
- Find how your life style relates to your work style.

THE CRYSTAL BALL IN YOUR BRAIN

This is an Insight Chapter. By understanding patterns you can get ready to make changes. The brain's most powerful tool is the imagination. People can see into the past, present, future—or into situations that will never actually happen.

Like any tool, imagination can be used for positive purposes, such as problem solving, or it can harm people if left uncontrolled. Imaginary images are often so strong that people's bodies react as though they were living through the actual experience of whatever at work demons the crystal ball in their brains is conjuring up.

When you're having a pleasant daydream or deliberately recalling a beautiful scene from nature to maintain a feeling of calm and tranquility, your body seems to float peacefully—energy flows from you easily. There are no abrupt physical changes, no stresses or strains. When your crystal ball suddenly clouds with dark images of negative or horrible outcomes (such as possibly getting fired or being publicly reprimanded by your supervisor), your body rockets into a red alert emergency. The pounding heart, rapid breathing, hand tremors, dry mouth—all or some of your habitual anxiety reactions—take hold of your body. Just like Dorothy in the *Wizard of Oz*, you are physically shocked when the image in the crystal ball changes from Aunty Em to the Wicked Witch.

JUMP OUT OF THE PLANE, NOW

Research has shown that most paratroopers used to have greater fears about falling than average people. They tended to have an unusual or irrational fear of heights. So why did they volunteer to join military units that regularly jump out of planes? Because they're counterphobic—they directly attack the thing they fear most. This counterattack is one possible response to the fight-flight reaction.

What can you learn from paratroopers? You can train yourself to jump into danger—at least in your imagination.

HORROR FILMS IN YOUR HEAD

Look at the items you rated or checked off in your anxiety inventories from Chapter 7. How many of these situations have you experienced directly and how many have you imagined? Memories of unpleasant work situations or imagined scenarios may haunt you, building anticipatory anxiety to an unbearable level. What can you do to make these anxiety-inducing situations go away?

Sit or lie down, close your eyes and relax, using the steps from Chapter 3. Now imagine one of the horror stories from work.

Form the most vivid image that you can. Pretend that it's actually happening, not that it will happen, but that it is happening. Let yourself experience as much of your usual anxiety reaction as you can. If it helps, speak aloud your part in any conversation. Make the worst happen in your work horror story and note how you feel. Spend a few minutes trying to feel the full fear reaction.

Open your eyes and calm yourself down.

Practice imagining all the work horror stories you indicated in earlier chapters (and maybe a few you didn't write down or check off) and let the worst happen in your imagination, using the calming steps of Chapter 3 whenever necessary.

It's Getting Better All the Time

Slowly, improve your horror stories. Don't let the worst happen. Gradually, make them less awful, less negative. After a few weeks, try changing the horror stories into success stories. Use your imagination to turn yourself into a hero.

Your boss begins shouting, "I should fire you for messing up the figures in that report!" You cut the boss off with, "Those figures are correct. Yours are the ones that are wrong. Besides, I quit. Your main competitor has hired me for a much higher salary."

By using your imagination to deal with the worst possibilities, you add strength to your psychological muscle tissue. As you improve your stories, you begin to deal with more likely scenarios, and start discovering some practical alternatives to your anxiety-driven behavior and responses. You begin to rehearse for success.

Reversal of Fortune

If the work horror stories were too unpleasant, try starting with success stories and slowly move toward negative work situations. Keep practicing until you're able to imagine the worst possible outcomes. Once you've visualized your horror stories, reverse your fortunes again gradually toward success. Be sure to write down any discoveries or ideas you might actually try at work to help you advance in your career or to deal with negative situations.

TIME OUT FOR AN IMAGINARY TOUR[1]

To start the imagination tour, sit or lie down again, and get as comfortable as possible. Relax and use the calming steps from Chapter 3. (Some people like to take this tour with a friend or family member who reads the directions, asks the questions, and writes down what they report. Others prefer to use a tape recorder or just work alone with the book.)

On this imagination tour (Assagioli 1976), close your eyes and visualize scenes, people, animals, or objects. Make images as vivid as possible and explore the surroundings. Notice as much as possible. Once the images are clear, spend a minute looking around before opening your eyes to follow the next direction. Close your eyes and regain the images again as needed.

First stop: a meadow.   Visualize yourself in a meadow. Describe in detail what you see below (use a separate sheet of paper, if necessary).

_____
_____
_____
_____
_____
_____
_____

When you need to, close your eyes and return to the image to answer the following questions.

Was there grass in the meadow? (If not, go back to the image and look for some.)

Describe the length and color of the grass. _____
_____
_____

---

[1] For an extended study of imagery interpretation, see Robert Assagioli, M.D., *Psychosynthesis: A Manual of Principles and Techniques* (New York: Penguin Books, 1976).

Is the sun shining? Describe the day (or night). _____

_____

_____

Second stop: climbing a mountain. Visualize yourself climbing a mountain. Describe in detail what you see below (use a separate sheet of paper, if necessary).

_____

_____

_____

_____

_____

_____

Close your eyes and return to the image, if necessary, to answer the following questions.

How high is the mountain? _____

Is it hard to climb? _____

If your mountain wasn't very high, look around for the highest one you can see and climb that one. How hard is it to climb?

_____

Third stop: following a stream. Visualize yourself following a stream. Describe in detail what you see below (use a separate sheet of paper, if necessary).

_____

_____

_____

_____

_____

_____

When you need to, close your eyes and return to the image to answer the following questions.

How fast does the water in the stream flow? _____

How deep is the water and how wide is the stream? _____

_____

Are there rocks or other objects blocking the stream? _____

_____

Fourth stop: a person.   Imagine you hear the name of someone of the same gender as you. Visualize that person. Describe her or him in detail. Tell what kind of personality he or she has below (use a separate sheet of paper, if necessary).

_____

_____

_____

_____

_____

_____

Fifth stop: some cattle.   Visualize yourself back in the meadow. One by one some cattle come into the meadow: a cow, a bull, and some calves. Describe what happens in detail. Tell how each one relates to you and to each other (use a separate sheet of paper, if necessary).

_____

_____

_____

_____

_____

_____

Sixth stop: volcanic eruption.   Visualize the eruption of a volcano. Describe what happens in detail (use a separate sheet of paper, if necessary).

_____

_____

_____

_____

_____

_____

Last stop: The lion.   Visualize a lion. Have the lion confront those at work who oppose you or block your advancement. Describe what happens in detail (use a separate sheet of paper, if necessary).

_____

_____

_____

_____

_____

_____

_____

Back to Work

Your imaginary tour should tell you something about how you approach situations in general and on the job.

Take each stop one by one.

A meadow.   If your meadow has tall and green grass with the sun shining brightly, you're generally feeling psychologically healthy and you're probably in good shape emotionally.

If your grass was short, you may be trying to control your emotions a little too much or using logic or rules in areas meant for fun or enjoyment. Too much control can wear you out even before you get to work.

No grass or little grass? Cloudy or rainy day or nighttime? Something is probably spoiling your general mood. If your sad or depressed mood is constant and unyielding, some professional counseling or therapy might help you. Sometimes depression just goes away, but your progress may be faster with professional treatment.

Climbing a mountain.   If your mountain is high or very large, you have high aspirations and ambitions. If it was also steep and difficult to climb, then you must find ways to lower your stress, or lower your aspirations.

A small mountain or hill shows that you've already achieved (or nearly achieved) all your ambitions and you see no reason to push yourself. If your mountain is also hard to climb, you may be having difficulty keeping up with your present job responsibilities. Is something unusual going on at work or at home? If you're overworked, ask your supervisor for some help.

A hill might also mean that too many people or things are holding you back. Reevaluate your ambitions. Where do you want to be five years from now?

Following a stream.   Your stream has to do with psychological energy. A fast-moving stream means you like to move or think fast. A slow one indicates that you usually need more time to get going.

Can you see to the bottom? Is the water clear? If so, you usually have clear insight into yourself and your problems. Nothing is hidden.

Rocks, logs, and other obstructions indicate that pessimistic thoughts, fears, and negative attitudes may be blocking your ability to use all your energy at work. You need to use your imagination to explore these obstructions more.

A person.   The same-gender person that you imagined is usually your ideal self. Compare this with the ideal that you developed from the cards in Chapter 4. Is this ideal self someone you'd really like to be more like? Then make his or her traits your goal. Try to be more like this ideal self.

Some cattle.   Don't be insulted, but these cattle scenes usually give a picture of a person's family (past or present). The cow is the mother, the bull is the father, and the calves are children, usually your brothers and/or sisters. How do you relate to each one? How do they relate to each other in your meadow?

Sometimes we inadvertently treat others at work as members of our family. Your attitudes and feelings toward your co-workers might really be transferred from your attitudes and feelings about your siblings. Were you afraid of an older brother or sister? Did a younger brother or sister provoke conflict and trouble for you?

Does anybody act like the at work cow or bull? Be careful: it's easy to treat supervisors or old-timers as though they were parental figures, and some supervisors enjoy the role.

Volcanic eruption.   How violent is your volcano? How long did it take to erupt? Was it easy or difficult for the eruption to begin? This scene deals with the amount of tension that usually builds up in you and the way you release it.

If your volcano is very violent and explosive, then you're storing up a lot of tension before releasing it. Don't wait so long to find relief. You don't necessarily have to release the tension violently, but stop waiting so long.

If it took awhile building up to the actual eruption, then you may be having trouble finding ways to release your tension. Unrelieved tension may easily turn to anxiety. Find ways to relax and release pent up feelings.

The lion.   Your lion usually shows how you deal with your opponents when expressing yourself. Does your lion attack your opponents or only roar? A retreating lion may indicate a too-timid attitude when dealing with opponents or competitors. You think opponents who run from your lion's roar should back down in a real confrontation. Is this true?

If your lion attacked and ate one of your opponents, is this natural for the lion's healthy appetite or is the lion hitting too hard because of fear? How does your lion operate at work?

TIME TRAVEL

Many of the paratroopers who feared falling had clear memories of falling during their childhoods. Maybe some of your early memories relate to your present day work anxieties.

8

Travel as far back in time as you can in your memories. Some people remember seeing a room from their cribs or playing with a toy or riding in a car. Others only remember important events like a birthday party or their first day at school. Take a few minutes (as many as 15 or 20 minutes) to remember and write down your first three memories (try to put them in order, but don't worry too much about which one was really first):

Early Memory One

_____

_____

_____

_____

_____

_____

_____

Early Memory Two

_____
_____
_____
_____
_____
_____
_____
_____
_____

Early Memory Three

_____
_____
_____
_____
_____
_____
_____
_____
_____

Your Life Work/Your Work Life

Somewhere in the pattern of your memories is your basic approach to life, the way you see yourself, and what you expect from situations like work (Adler 1964). Out of years of various experiences, you chose to remember these particular events. It was no accident. These memories express your fundamental goals, who or what helps or obstructs you, and perhaps even why you experience anxiety on the job. Think about how these memories relate to your present life and career situation.

1. Who (besides yourself) is in these memories?

_____
_____

2. How do the other people in these memories relate to you? Does anything similar happen now at work or at home?

_____
_____

3. Are you a victim, a hero, or an observer? How active are you in these memories?

_____

_____

Don't be discouraged if you cannot find how these early memories immediately relate to your life and work situations. Be on the lookout for any resemblances. Remember that most solutions to problems suddenly appear to prepared minds. The insight you've begun to get from this chapter will help you know solutions when you see them.

8

Chapter Checkpoints

✓ Imagination is a person's most powerful problem-solving tool.

✓ People sometimes counterattack what they fear.

✓ Use horror films in your head to prepare for the worst and the best.

9 | Putting Anxiety to Work

This chapter will help you to:

- Start converting anxious energy into mass.
- Work off nervous energy.
- Assert with I statements.

This is an action chapter. Here you'll put into action what you've discovered in previous chapters. If you've been taking the surveys in the inventory chapters, working through the exercises in the insight chapters, and following the steps in Chapters 3 and 6, then you:

- Know what situations at work cause anxiety.
- Can recognize your usual anxiety reactions.
- Know that fear reactions are normal.
- Have learned to change your responses to anxiety at work.
- Have become an expert on your own work anxiety.
- Have attacked anxiety physically.
- Have attacked anxiety psychologically.
- Have attacked anxiety practically.
- Have developed new strategies for dealing with anxiety.
- Have begun to overcome anxiety's negative effects at work.

ANXIOUS ENERGY JUMP STARTS OTHER EMOTIONS

Anxious energy often gets channelled into other emotions. Anger, being an especially close relative of anxiety from the fight-flight reaction, is the most typical emotional channel for anxious energy, but there are others. Adults sometimes start giggling or acting silly in the presence of those whose behavior is obviously strange, but not because they're amused. Such bizarre behavior triggers a laugh fueled by fear.

Actors, who must master their emotional reactions, learn to use their stage fright to put an emotional edge into their acting. They push their anxious energy into the emotions of rage, anger, sadness, or happiness— whatever their acting scene demands. You can do the same with your anxious feelings.

Practice acting. Pretend that you're only acting your role in a play or movie on your job. When you become anxious, try to make the energy fit your part. Try acting happier or livelier or more commanding, if that seems appropriate. Experiment with anxious energy.

TURNING FEAR INTO INTEREST

Remember that states of anxiety are closely related to states of general arousal or interest. One measure of aroused interest and excitement, and of anxiety as well, is the dilation of the pupils of the eyes. The pupils open wide (getting up to 30 times larger) to take in more light when we're interested in or frightened of what we see. Our pupils constrict when we're faced with unpleasant scenes (for which we have no fear) or when we see things that have no interest for us (McCutcheon 1989).

A boss that frightens you already has your attention, and you can bet that your pupils dilate whenever he or she walks toward your worksite or desk. Why not try turning your body's reaction around? Your eyes are wide open. Start studying your boss. Notice everything about your boss that you can. Learn everything about your boss that you can. Encourage him or her to talk about personal experiences, likes and dislikes.

You may not succeed in making your boss your favorite subject, but you'll learn some interesting things and you'll become less anxious. Where will the anxious energy go? Probably back into your work.

Try turning fear into interest in other work situations. This will go a long way toward reducing anxiety. Afraid of making spelling or grammatical errors in the memos that you type or prepare? If you turn this fear into intense interest in English, its history, and grammar, you may find that knowledge will take the edge off your fears.

CONVERTING ENERGY BACK TO MASS

Remember Einstein's formula: $E = mc^2$, where E is energy, m is mass, and c is the speed of light.

You're not really going to reverse Einstein's formula. Instead, take your anxious energy and use it to do massive amounts of physical work.

At every worksite and office, there are always projects left undone (or waiting to the last minute). Objects have to be relocated, floors have to be cleared or cleaned, files have to be sorted and stored away, and photocopies have to be made or collated. Your own workstation, work vehicle, desk, or workbench, is probably overdue for some cleaning, moving, maintenance, or adjustment.

When you're feeling full of anxious energy, start on these projects. Keep that energy flowing from you into massive work projects. And when you're finished with your area, look for other areas to work on. (Avoid spending your whole day on such projects, complete them on a break from more stressful tasks.) Sometimes a ten-minute massive project workout can get you mentally prepared for your regular job duties.

If nothing else is available, take a walk to the most distant part of the worksite or office area that you can reasonably visit. Meet with another employee at the other end of the building for some legitimate reason. Offer to run errands or drop things off. Find ways to burn up energy.

Jogging or running may not be for you, but if you can manage some sort of exercise program for yourself, your anxiety levels are sure to drop. Even a brisk lunchtime walk can help get your body back into a comfortable rhythm again.

Almost any moderate physical exercise, done on a regular basis, will enable you to regulate your anxiety better. If you have physical or medical limitations, consult a physician about what exercises are most appropriate.

FEAR OF ANGER

You may have learned (or even been trained) to react with fear to your anger. When confronted with an angry customer or co-worker, you may be getting scared twice—once by your confronter and again by your dangerous anger.

Just as anxiety is a natural reaction, so is anger. Both originated in the fight-flight reaction, and one can change to the other easily.

Some experts believe that the fight option from the fight-flight reaction is more accurately described as defensive attack. Cornered animals demonstrate the defensive nature of such attacks when they turn to fight against overwhelming odds.

You might feel cornered almost all the time in the competitiveness of the workplace, ready to blurt out verbal attacks when provoked by co-workers or supervisors. You may even feel duty bound to put down aggressive or unfair employees. You may find yourself holding in your anxious anger until it explodes in a foolish attack.

Some people are so uncomfortable with anxious feelings that they attack their fears (just like those who join the paratroopers to conquer their fear of falling). Nobody enjoys feeling afraid. People resent their fears, and resent those who make them feel afraid. Sooner or later (sooner for those of us who act counterphobically) people launch a defensive attack.

ASSERT, DON'T ATTACK

Leon, the company clown, stops by to tell his latest off-color story. The female workers nearby consider his jokes offensive and bordering on sexual harassment, but they don't say anything. You've tried to discourage him by teasing him about his gross jokes, but he seems to have a new joke every day.

You're starting to get angry, and soon you'll explode with a personal attack on Leon. It might even get physical.

Don't attack, assert your rights. Instead of saying, "You stupid so and so . . . ," say, "Leon, I don't think this is the right place for your stories. They're making the women here uncomfortable, and I wish you'd wait until later to tell your buddy the latest joke."

If Leon persists, usually you'll get support from others, but even if you don't, restate your wishes in an objective, assertive way. Say, "Leon, I don't want to become upset or angry. Why don't you just save that story until later? Let it go for now." If Leon still doesn't stop, say, "I don't want to make this a big deal, Leon, but I'll have to report this to the supervisor."

You may have to physically leave the area. Even if your colleagues don't say anything, some or all of them will leave with you, diminishing Leon's audience. Chances are, Leon's off-color jokes will soon cease, if he's met with assertiveness.

Attackers say "You"—Asserters Say "I"

Attacking someone consists of casting blame, making accusations, name-calling, starting rumors, sabotaging the person's work, reporting every mistake, and sometimes throwing objects or fists. These are clearly attacks, directed at a person.

Typical attacks involve shouting such as: "You deliberately left me off the lunch list!" "You made me look foolish by changing the figures at the last minute." "You did that to get me angry." "You're making it hard for me to do my job."

What you usually get back when you launch an attack is a counterattack: "You're the one who claimed to be on a diet." "I can't help it if you're too lazy or stupid to read the final report before the meeting." "You're crazy." "You're just incompetent."

Instead, be assertive by stating (as objectively as possible) what you like or dislike and what you want the other employee (or your boss) to do or not do. You might say, "I expected to be on the lunch list. Please add my name." Or, "I didn't like being left off the lunch list. Please add me next time." "I don't like to look foolish. Please warn me the next time if changes are made." "I got upset when you put that pipe cutter on my clean shirt. I'd like you to pay the cleaning bill." "I spent forty-five minutes searching for those computer disks. Please don't borrow anything from my desk, without asking me first, okay?"

Assert, Don't Settle

Sometimes we have to surrender to the situation and settle for exactly what a supervisor or a co-worker wants, but not always. Fellow employees, including the top management, can sometimes make unreasonable demands or enforce unfair rules or procedures, or even break the rules. They may put you and other workers in jeopardy, or make things uncomfortable.

If you're in the habit of acting passive, it's time to turn and assert, not attack. When you're overworked, say, "I don't think I'll be able to complete this new task without some help." Or, "If this is a priority, then I'll need someone to take over the County Works Project." Or, "I don't feel that it is fair to add this new responsibility to my department when it clearly should be done by the Manufacturing Team."

Assertion Rules

1. Try to do what's right. When you're asserting yourself, try to do what's best in the work situation. You're not just asserting your rights. Remain helpful and clear about your job responsibilities.
2. Avoid blaming. People spend too much time blaming others and deflecting blame from themselves. Everybody makes mistakes. Let them drop. Accept some responsibility if necessary but move on to problem solving.
3. Change attacks to statements of fact. When you attack someone personally, then that person usually counterattacks. Instead, say objectively what you want or feel in an I statement. Doing so encourages the other employee to respond more objectively.
4. Set limits or conditions. Be as helpful as you can at work. Always be ready to help think of better ways to get the job done. In a minor emergency you may be willing to sacrifice some of your free time. Set limits and state what conditions you expect when working on your regular job tasks or on special projects.
5. Don't let important issues slide. If something about your work is bothering you, express it in an I statement to your supervisor. For example: "My doctor says that I can't really wait until 2 P.M. to break for lunch. With my stomach condition, I need to take lunch no later than 1 P.M. Starting Monday, I am going to take lunch at 12 or 1, which do you prefer?"
6. Make solutions, not just complaints. Keep assertions as positive as possible. Try to think of alternatives to the present problem. See if you can work something out that makes everybody happy and gets the job done.

Practice Time

On the following lines write three "you" attack complaints about your co-workers or supervisors. Then write an I statement that will change the situation for the better.

Attack	I Statement
1. _____	_____
_____	_____
_____	_____
2. _____	_____
_____	_____
_____	_____
3. _____	_____
_____	_____
_____	_____

9

Chapter Checkpoints

✓ Anxious energy is energy you can use to act more assertively or to become more alert.

✓ Fear can change to interest—this dispels anxiety.

✓ Anxiety can be worked off in useful ways.

✓ Acting assertively can head off anxious feelings.

✓ Using I statements works better than "you" attacks.

CHAPTER

10 | Conquering the Worst Anxieties

This chapter will help you to:

- Handle supervisors, interviews, speeches, promotions, and deadlines.
- Learn problem-specific techniques to address anxiety.
- Overcome getting fired.

In this applications chapter, apply the I-I-A process to seven common anxiety-provoking situations at work.

TYRANNICAL SUPERVISOR OR CO-WORKERS

Overly aggressive and dominant employees think nothing of mentally or physically invading another worker's space. Sometimes, they seek and hold positions of authority, legitimizing their invasions. They also tend to be demanding and overcritical of their co-workers, subordinates, and superiors. They insist on getting their way and persist even when their ideas are shown to be impractical. Loving a good fight, they must win— at almost all costs. Tyrants like this often forget about whomever they hurt or whatever mistakes they made, so appealing to the past has little effect on them.

With these types of people, avoid confrontations or blaming contests, because they insist on winning and no progress will be made. Use the assertion rules from Chapter 9 and appeal to improving the efficiency of the work situation and to plans for future projects. Mildly threaten that work might not get done, which will reflect badly on the whole department or work crew. Make a deal. Tyrants love deals if they think they're getting a good one.

Use the Inventory-Insight-Action process on tyrants you must work with. Make a list of what the tyrant does—good and bad. Try to learn as much as you can about him or her. Find patterns in behavior. Think of ways to become more helpful to this type of colleague while planning a strategy to limit his or her intrusive power. Deliberately seek regular communication.

When the time is right, assert yourself. Tell what you want and state your limits or conditions. Be ready to make a deal by having one ready. Negotiate.

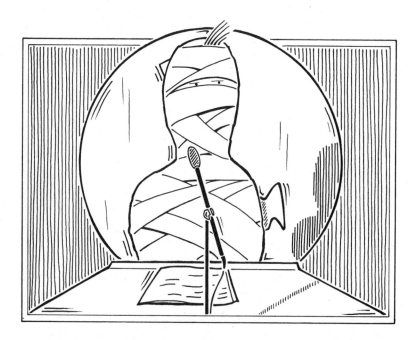

PETRIFYING PRESENTATIONS

Speaking to large groups (or even to small ones) can turn dynamic people into mummies. People fear they will freeze like a deer caught in the headlights of an oncoming car, suddenly unable to speak. They also fear fainting, stuttering, or blurting out garbled words—in general, acting like a total fool.

That's the risk one takes when speaking publicly. That's why it's an act of courage. It is scary. There is, however, a lot more risk driving on a highway.

Overcome Your Speaking Fears

Here are seven tips that will help you become a better speaker.

1. *Know your stuff.* If you know your material, then you're doing your audience a favor by speaking to them. You're saving them time and effort (and maybe even money). Don't forget that they need you. What you have to say is more valuable for them to hear than for you to say. Make a list of what you already know and what you need to learn. Then go outside of the topic area to see if there's something especially interesting you can bring to your speech, something a little different.

2. *Tell the audience what you're going to talk about, talk about it, then tell them what you talked about.* This simple outline has been used successfully by thousands of speakers. Keep your presentation short. If you have a maximum of 10 minutes, try to use only 5.

3. *Use your memory, with help from notes or index cards if you need it, but don't read your speech* (except for small segments that are direct quotes or are difficult to remember). If you know your material, your presentation will be easier on the audience.

4. *Admit your stage fright.* Find a simple or humorous way to admit that you're uncomfortable or afraid to speak in public. Sometimes a small joke will do the trick. Drink a glass of water (without any ice) just as you begin to speak. Say something like: "I had the ice taken out of this water so you wouldn't hear it rattle as my hand shook." You might even shake the glass a little, but not enough to spill water. Or, deliberately shake a glass of water with ice to make it rattle, saying, "It's a good thing I'm not nervous this morning."

5. *Speak conversationally and refer to the here-and-now, not just to the topic of your speech.* Make a comment about the weather, a noise from the back of the room, the city you're in, the color of the carpet—anything to reduce the formality of your speech. Your tension and the audience's will be considerably lowered if you make a natural everyday observation.

6. *Breathe deeply and slow down.* Take deep breaths as you speak and stop yourself from speeding up. Directly ask your audience a question if you find yourself going too fast.

7. *Practice, practice, practice.* Practice your speech in front of friends, in front of the mirror, to your children and pets, to a tape recorder or video camera. Push yourself to give presentations (short ones at first) and work your way up to speeches before large audiences.

10

Use the anxiety-reduction steps from the earlier chapters. Once you've given a few speeches, you'll begin to enjoy talking to large groups, even if you still get a little nervous.

NIGHTMARE ALLEY PROMOTIONS

There's an old Tyrone Power movie called *Nightmare Alley*, where the hero (mainly through trickery) achieves a position that he can't handle. He gets outfoxed and falls into a nightmare alley existence. Some characters say he reached too high.

If you've suddenly been promoted way over your head, immediately take stock (inventory) of your job responsibilities, resources, and options. Make a list of each and of the names and job responsibilities of those you supervise.

If you're unfamiliar with a new area or department (and you've become the boss), speak to each of your employees, one at a time. See which ones are willing to show you the ropes. Beware of people who know it all; they, more than likely, resent that you got "their" promotion and may deliberately try to undermine you.

Get an organizational chart of your company. Learn where you and your department fit in. Make your own chart of employees' work flow and their relation to other departments. Be clear about what your supervisor wants. Give top priority to whatever your supervisor wants: make sure those specific jobs get done.

Sign up for management seminars that are held on weekends or on two weeknights. Enroll in some college courses, if you can.

Find a manager at your level who's willing to make suggestions. Your immediate supervisor is probably the wrong choice. Don't admit right away that you can't handle your assignment. Maybe you can, if you give yourself a chance.

INTERVIEWS

Next to public speaking, interviews (going to them and giving them) are probably the most anxiety-provoking work situations there are.

Whether you are going on an interview or conducting one, good preparation is the best way to reduce anxious feelings. As the interviewer, you should have standard questions prepared, and standard answers ready about job responsibilities and benefits. You also need to have a salary range as a guide, in case you find a perfect candidate. Some managers like to use an interview form with questions and responses that they can check off or write comments on. Always spend a few minutes reviewing a candidate's application or résumé before admitting him or her to your office, even if you must make the job candidate wait.

If you're the job candidate, do your homework. Learn what you can about the organization that you are trying to join. The more ignorant you are about a firm or institution, the more vulnerable you are during the interview.

Make sure your résumé is completely updated and professional. Sloppy, outdated, and poorly photocopied résumés usually wind up in the trash. Make sure your appearance is as neat and professional as that of other employees in the company.

Make a list of likely interview questions and write good solid answers to each one. Learn to recite a few routine sentences about yourself and your skills. Practice with your friends and family (a tape or video recording also works well). Find an answer for this trick question: "What is your greatest weakness and how do you intend to overcome it?" Make your weakness a strength that you'll try to tone down a bit for the sake of other workers.

Show that you've been listening to the interviewer by asking for a clarification of some point that he or she has made. Ask a question about the probationary period, vacation time, or health insurance. Avoid simple yes or no answers, but don't start chattering on nervously either. Try to explain the kind of work and the kinds of problems you handled on your last job.

Use the steps in the earlier chapters to help reduce your anxious feelings. Make a horror story (from Chapter 8) about an upcoming interview. Then gradually turn it into a success story.

OUTSIDE DISTRACTIONS

Accept life-and-death calls from home. Otherwise, limit calls to one call a day at lunch time or quitting time. Do everything possible to avoid invasions from your home life into your work life. Have contingency plans to cover most predictable home crises, such as back-up child care.

10

Problems at home can damage your work performance, so you can't simply ignore them. Seek professional help for serious physical or psychological difficulties. If you're showing up at work late or disoriented, take your supervisor into your confidence. Perhaps you need a leave of absence to settle your home crisis.

DEAD LAST—LATE AGAIN

In most organizations, tardy employees are viewed as negligent at best. Supervisors suspect that late employees really hate their jobs or only care about collecting paychecks, not doing work.

First, do an inventory of how many times you've been late over the last two weeks—and by how much. Next, answer honestly whether or not you hate your job or your supervisor. Is a second job or night activity cutting into your sleep time? Are you secretly hoping to get fired? Do you feel that you are a victim. Are you angry at your company? Do you feel the company owes you something? Are you getting revenge for some injury?

Whether you've answered these questions yes or no, take steps to stop being late.

If you need to find another job, falling down on this one won't help. Make special transportation arrangements, if necessary. Get up an hour earlier. Do whatever is necessary to get to work *early*.

If missed deadlines are your problem, do a similar inventory. Investigate your feelings. Are your assignments impossible to complete on time without help? Speak directly to your supervisor about getting help. Tell him or her that it's not possible and suggest alternatives.

Give yourself enough lead time. Stay after work the first night you get a new assignment, if you can, and give yourself a head start.

TERMINATION

The worst has happened. Suddenly, no one wants your skills. You have no value. You've been cancelled like a check that's already been cashed. You feel worthless. None of this is really true.

Losing your job is only the end of one phase of your career and the beginning of another. It's a forced opportunity that you need to make the most of.

Prepare yourself for a great adventure and a terrible ordeal: hope, disappointment, depression, and even ridicule. Get ready for a long siege, because it may take months to find a good job again.

Plan for an immediate attack on your problem. Make a list of what you'll need to find a new job: a new résumé, some new clothes, perhaps a special budget. Gather job sources and make a list of contacts. Train yourself for many, many interviews.

Most importantly, maintain faith in your abilities and faith that one day soon you'll be in the right place at the right time, or that a friend will help you get your foot in the door of a good organization.

As long as you keep actively searching for work, you are entitled to all the basic rights and benefits you've always enjoyed. Although you may have to cut back on some expenses, do not allow anyone to treat you as a second-class citizen. Defend your right to be respected, and do not allow home chores to interfere in any way with your job search. Do not accept inappropriate family chores just because you feel guilty about not working.

Get tough. Mentally prepare yourself for rejection. Unless you're lucky or your skill is in high demand, chances are you'll be turned down for jobs—some that you don't even want. Depression may become your biggest enemy.

10

Use the anxiety-reduction steps in the earlier chapters to stop yourself from worrying. Keep planning and talking to people. Check your job sources every day and if your unemployment benefits run out, seek out temporary agencies to help find interim work. Don't give up.

Chapter Checkpoints

✓ You can learn to relate effectively to most overly aggressive bosses and co-workers.

✓ Giving presentations is a matter of preparation, practice, courage, and the use of special techniques.

✓ You can learn to rise to the occasion of being promoted beyond your experience.

✓ Interviews go better with perfect preparation and practice.

✓ Take inventory of your tardiness or missed deadlines—then start being early.

Post-Test

How are you progressing in overcoming anxiety? Wait at least two weeks after you've finished the exercises in this book before answering these 25 questions. For each question, give a score for yourself at home and another score for yourself at work.

Score four, when your answer is frequently or always.

Score two, when your answer is sometimes.

Score zero, when your answer is never or almost never.

	At Home	At Work
Group I. I feel confident when:		
1. I'm late.	_____	_____
2. I might make a mistake.	_____	_____
3. I'm being criticized.	_____	_____
4. I'm being watched while working.	_____	_____
5. I think about losing control.	_____	_____
Subtotals	_____	_____

	At Home	At Work
Group II. I feel confident when:		
6. Speaking to those in authority.	_____	_____
7. Speaking to a small group.	_____	_____
8. Speaking to a large group.	_____	_____
9. Speaking on the telephone.	_____	_____
10. Speaking to strangers.	_____	_____
Subtotals	_____	_____

	At Home	At Work
Group III. I feel confident when:		
11. I get angry.	_____	_____
12. Confronting those who are negligent.	_____	_____
13. Dealing with bossy people.	_____	_____
14. Dealing with angry people.	_____	_____
15. Thinking about being attacked.	_____	_____
Subtotals	_____	_____

	At Home	At Work
Group IV. I feel confident when:		
16. I have to change a routine or plan.	_____	_____
17. Thinking about injury or illness.	_____	_____
18. Taking on new responsibilities.	_____	_____
19. Meeting deadlines.	_____	_____
20. Learning to use new equipment.	_____	_____
Subtotals	_____	_____

	At Home	At Work
Group V. I feel confident when:		
21. I'm surrounded by a crowd.	_____	_____
22. I'm completely alone.	_____	_____
23. I'm in enclosed places.	_____	_____
24. I hear a sudden loud noise.	_____	_____
25. I hear sirens.	_____	_____
Subtotals	_____	_____
At Home	**At Work**	
Total scores	_____	_____

These questions are the same ones that you scored at the beginning of the book except that the word *confident* has replaced *anxious*. Earlier, a high total score or a high subtotal indicated areas of home life or work life that were causing trouble. Now, a high score identifies areas that you handle well or may have even mastered.

RANGES OF CONFIDENCE

Total scores of 92 to 100 at work are exceptionally high.   You are ready to expand your job responsibilities, perhaps as a supervisor or department manager. You have almost completely mastered anxiety problems.

Total scores of 72 to 90 at work are moderately high.   Functioning at a high level is not a problem for you. If your job has minimal responsibilities, now is the time to push for something better. Volunteer to work on a new project or ask for a transfer to another department. Seek additional training or college credits to qualify yourself for advancement. Lingering doubts should not be allowed to hold you back. Take action and your confidence will continue to grow.

Total scores of 50 to 70 at work are moderate.   Although all areas of work are not yet completely comfortable for you, you have enough confidence to handle most situations well. By continuing to practice the I-I-A process, your confidence level will gradually increase. Progress may be slow, but if you keep pushing yourself, you'll improve steadily. Set limited goals and then take action.

Total scores below 50 at work are low.   Anxiety and lack of confidence are still acting as barriers to your success at work. Try going through all the exercises once more in the book. If that fails, perhaps you're in the wrong profession or in the wrong organization. A low at home score as well would indicate that work may not be the actual source of your trouble.

At Home Scores

At home scores should be higher than the at work ones. If not, you may be suffering from a tense or problem-filled home life. If particular at home subtotals are low, consider getting family counseling or other help that may alleviate these problem areas.

Group Subtotals

Those group areas with low scores or even zeroes will require more work, using the I-I-A process. Even more detailed progress can be gauged by comparing each question of this Post-Test inventory with the corresponding question on the Self-Assessment (Preliminary Anxiety Reading).

Review, Review, Review

Anxiety is never entirely overcome. Anxiety is always with us and may appear in slightly altered forms any time we face the unfamiliar. Periodically review *Overcoming Anxiety at Work*. Use the Skill Maintenance checklist inside the back cover to see if you're making progress (or at least maintaining the progress you've made).

Anxiety Date Book

To keep track of progress in the Anxiety Olympic training programs, use a separate notebook or journal as an anxiety date book rather than the one supplied. In any case, take the time to mark results, so that progress is clear. Use additional blank pages.

Program One

Date _____ Steps Attempted _____ Steps Completed _____

Date _____ Steps Attempted _____ Steps Completed _____

Date _____ Steps Attempted _____ Steps Completed _____

Date _____ Steps Attempted _____ Steps Completed _____

Date _____ Steps Attempted _____ Steps Completed _____

Date _____ Steps Attempted _____ Steps Completed _____

Date _____ Steps Attempted _____ Steps Completed _____

Date _____ Steps Attempted _____ Steps Completed _____

Date _____ Steps Attempted _____ Steps Completed _____

Date _____ Steps Attempted _____ Steps Completed _____

Date _____ Steps Attempted _____ Steps Completed _____

Date _____ Steps Attempted _____ Steps Completed _____

Date _____ Steps Attempted _____ Steps Completed _____

Date _____ Steps Attempted _____ Steps Completed _____

Date _____ Steps Attempted _____ Steps Completed _____

Date _____ Steps Attempted _____ Steps Completed _____

Use blank sheets.

Program Two

Date _____ Steps Attempted _____ Steps Completed _____

Date _____ Steps Attempted _____ Steps Completed _____

Date _____ Steps Attempted _____ Steps Completed _____

Date _____ Steps Attempted _____ Steps Completed _____

Date _____ Steps Attempted _____ Steps Completed _____

Date _____ Steps Attempted _____ Steps Completed _____

Date _____ Steps Attempted _____ Steps Completed _____

Date _____ Steps Attempted _____ Steps Completed _____

Date _____ Steps Attempted _____ Steps Completed _____

Date _____ Steps Attempted _____ Steps Completed _____

Date _____ Steps Attempted _____ Steps Completed _____

Date _____ Steps Attempted _____ Steps Completed _____

Date _____ Steps Attempted _____ Steps Completed _____

Date _____ Steps Attempted _____ Steps Completed _____

Date _____ Steps Attempted _____ Steps Completed _____

Date _____ Steps Attempted _____ Steps Completed _____

Use blank sheets.

Program Three

Date _____ Steps Attempted _____ Steps Completed _____

Date _____ Steps Attempted _____ Steps Completed _____

Date _____ Steps Attempted _____ Steps Completed _____

Date _____ Steps Attempted _____ Steps Completed _____

Date _____ Steps Attempted _____ Steps Completed _____

Date _____ Steps Attempted _____ Steps Completed _____

Date _____ Steps Attempted _____ Steps Completed _____

Date _____ Steps Attempted _____ Steps Completed _____

Date _____ Steps Attempted _____ Steps Completed _____

Date _____ Steps Attempted _____ Steps Completed _____

Date _____ Steps Attempted _____ Steps Completed _____

Date _____ Steps Attempted _____ Steps Completed _____

Date _____ Steps Attempted _____ Steps Completed _____

Date _____ Steps Attempted _____ Steps Completed _____

Date _____ Steps Attempted _____ Steps Completed _____

Use blank sheets.

Sort Cards

CUT OUT OR COPY

1. POSITIVE	2. ORGANIZED
3. PUNCTUAL	4. CREATIVE
5. CONFIDENT	6. NERVOUS
7. WORRIED	8. AFRAID

CUT OUT OR COPY

9. SHY	10. MOODY
11. AMBITIOUS	12. SLOPPY
13. TRUSTWORTHY	14. GENEROUS
15. FLEXIBLE	16. RIGID

CUT OUT OR COPY

17. COURAGEOUS	18. DECEITFUL
19. LAZY	20. CALM
21. HELPFUL	22. ENVIOUS
23. STUBBORN	24. SELFISH

CUT OUT OR COPY

25. HYPOCRITICAL	26. INSIGHTFUL
27. INCOMPETENT	28. HUMOROUS
29. INTOLERANT	30. HARDWORKING

SUGGESTED READING AND BIBLIOGRAPHY

Adler, Alfred. *The Individual Psychology of Alfred Adler*. Edited by H. Ansbacher. Harper Torchbooks, New York, 1964.

Assagioli, Roberto. *Psychosynthesis*. Penguin Books, New York, 1976.

Bettelheim, Bruno. *The Uses of Enchantment*. Alfred A. Knopf, New York, 1976.

Frankl, Viktor. *The Doctor and the Soul: From Psychotherapy to Logotherapy*. Vintage Books, New York, 1986.

Harris, Marvin. *Our Kind*. Harper & Row, New York, 1989.

Konner, Melvin. *Why the Reckless Survive*. Penguin Books, New York, 1990.

Lewis, H. W. *Technological Risk*. W. W. Norton & Company, New York, 1990.

McCutcheon, Marc. *The Compass in Your Nose*. Jeremy P. Tarcher, Inc., Los Angeles, 1989.

May, Robert. *Sex and Fantasy: Patterns of Male and Female Development*. Wide View, Boston, 1980.

Nicholi, Armand, ed. *The New Harvard Guide to Psychiatry*. Harvard University Press, Cambridge, 1988.

And works by:

Joseph Campbell

Erik Erikson

Sigmund Freud

Erich Fromm

Karen Horney

Carl G. Jung

Rollo May

THE BUSINESS SKILLS EXPRESS SERIES

This growing series of books addresses a broad range of key business skills and topics to meet the needs of employees, human resource departments, and training consultants.

To obtain information about these and other Business Skills Express books, please call Business One IRWIN toll free at: 1-800-634-3966.

Effective Performance Management	ISBN	1-55623-867-3
Hiring the Best	ISBN	1-55623-865-7
Writing that Works	ISBN	1-55623-856-8
Customer Service Excellence	ISBN	1-55623-969-6
Writing for Business Results	ISBN	1-55623-854-1
Powerful Presentation Skills	ISBN	1-55623-870-3
Meetings that Work	ISBN	1-55623-866-5
Effective Teamwork	ISBN	1-55623-880-0
Time Management	ISBN	1-55623-888-6
Assertiveness Skills	ISBN	1-55623-857-6
Motivation at Work	ISBN	1-55623-868-1
Overcoming Anxiety at Work	ISBN	1-55623-869-X
Positive Politics at Work	ISBN	1-55623-879-7
Telephone Skills at Work	ISBN	1-55623-858-4
Managing Conflict at Work	ISBN	1-55623-890-8
The New Supervisor: Skills for Success	ISBN	1-55623-762-6
The *Americans with Disabilities Act*: What Supervisors Need to Know	ISBN	1-55623-889-4